# THE POCKET GUIDE TO
# EQUINE KNOTS

# THE POCKET GUIDE TO
# EQUINE KNOTS

## A STEP-BY-STEP GUIDE TO THE MOST IMPORTANT KNOTS FOR HORSE AND RIDER

### DAN AADLAND

Skyhorse Publishing

Skyhorse Publishing books may be purchased in bulk at special
discounts for sales promotion, corporate gifts, fund-raising,
or educational purposes. Special editions can also be created
to specifications. For details, contact the Special Sales
Department, Skyhorse Publishing, 307 West 36th Street, 11th
Floor, New York, NY 10018 or info@skyhorsepublishing.com.

Skyhorse® and Skyhorse Publishing® are registered trademarks
of Skyhorse Publishing, Inc.®, a Delaware corporation.

Visit our website at www.skyhorsepublishing.com.

10 9 8 7 6

Library of Congress Cataloging-in-Publication Data
is available on file.

Cover design by Tom Lau
Cover photo credit: iStock.com

Print ISBN: 978-1-5107-1434-2
Ebook ISBN: 978-1-5107-1437-3

Printed in China

To my many equine mentors, particularly my father-in-law Elmer Johnson and my wife Emily. It was Elmer who taught me that no horseman should go through life ignorant of the bowline.

# CONTENTS

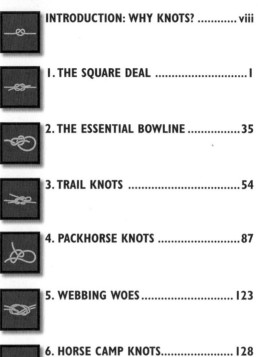

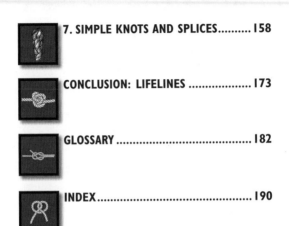

# INTRODUCTION: WHY KNOTS?

In an age of devices and gadgets intended to make life easier for us (but sometimes having the opposite effect), a horse lover may ask, "Why knots?" Why, in this day and age, is there a need for the ancient art of manipulating a piece of rope into various twists and turns to create this or that knot, hitch, or splice? Can't it all be done with buckles, snaps, and Velcro? Why take time to practice tying a bowline, a square knot, or a half hitch?

That question was answered for me many decades ago by a mare named Rosie and a mentor named Elmer (who became my father-in-law). Rosie was a powerful quarter horse mare sold to us by a young woman headed for college on a budget that didn't include continued board for the horse in a nearby city. The mare had been informally raced, had run barrels, and was well trained, she neck reined beautifully, and she lifted effortlessly from her trot to a canter she could seemingly hold all day. Lacking experience with cows, she took to them readily, and although a little quirky and spooky, she soon earned her keep on the ranch. That bay mare became the first horse I could call my own.

But Rosie had a fault. She pulled back. She was one of those inveterate pullers occasionally encountered in the equine world, and she'd break anything you used to restrain her. Tie her up with halter and lead rope and she'd lunge back so hard and so suddenly that something—the lead rope, the snap, the halter itself—would break. And, if her halter and lead rope were stronger than the object to which she was tied, she'd break the post or hitching rail. Then Rosie would calmly start grazing, making it clear what she'd had in mind.

This was a serious fault for a ranch horse, and the velocity with which she threw her twelve hundred pounds backward also made it a danger, both to herself and to anyone or anything behind her. How would I keep her in one place while I set irrigation water or fixed fence? In the open West, failing to hold onto your horse can mean a long, hot walk home.

Elmer had seen a few horses "spoiled" in this fashion and said we'd try to cure her, though he was dubious about the result. He explained that someone had tied her poorly while she was a colt. She'd probably spooked, pulled, broken free, found reward in tasty nearby grass, then tried it again, eventually finding that if she pulled hard enough, something would break and release her. (I have to wonder what Elmer would have thought of the "breakaway" tying systems marketed today that actually *train* a horse to be rewarded by pulling back—but that's another story.)

"I'm thinking that if she once came up against something she absolutely could not break, maybe she'd figure it out and quit. I'm not too hopeful, but we'll give it a try." With that, Elmer got into the Jeep and headed for town, while I continued my barn chores. He soon returned and displayed a coil of ¾-inch nylon rope. "There isn't a horse alive that can break this stuff. You can pull a pickup out of the barrow pit with it."

"But do we have a halter strong enough?"

"We won't use one. We'll tie it around her neck." I had visions of a strangling horse, and Elmer read my mind. "I'll use a bowline, and that's the *only* knot that won't tighten up and will still allow us to get it untied, no matter how hard she pulls." I'd heard of bowlines, probably reading of such a knot in the books in the seafaring section of the county library, all of which I'd read. But I didn't know how to tie one.

Elmer tied the soft, braided nylon rope around Rosie's neck, his fingers fluid, the motion too quick for me to follow construction of the knot. Then he led Rosie to a snubbing post in the middle of the corral, a post made of a railroad tie set deeply into the ground. After he tied another bowline around the post, we both stepped back. Rosie stood there a few seconds, backed slightly until slack was gone from the rope, then exploded. Dust flew while she snorted, strained, and repeatedly threw her weight and muscle back against the unyielding nylon rope.

But Elmer, soft-hearted man that he was, couldn't stand it. After fifteen or twenty seconds, he slipped in quickly with his pocket knife and cut the rope. "I couldn't watch her do that. She'd have pulled every muscle in her body. You'll have to use the hobbles, Dan."

I watched as Elmer untied the rope from around Rosie's neck, amazed that he could so easily untie a knot that had just withstood repeated lunges from a heavy animal, and amazed, too, that the noose hadn't tightened the slightest bit. It was clear Elmer had cut the rope only for his safety—he didn't want to be between a thrashing animal and the snubbing post.

No, we didn't "cure" Rosie. Luckily, she was a sucker for hobbles, never learning to hop or run in them as some horses do. I could slip the rawhide hobbles on her front pasterns, fix fence or do some other chore, and she'd graze nearby, moving at most with baby steps.

But I learned to tie a bowline. Without it, how could I safely tie a horse that had lost its halter? How could I tie a rope to the front axle of the tractor to pull it out of the mud and still be able to untie the knot rather than ruin the rope by cutting it loose? The Rosie incident had made it clear to me that horsemanship consists of more than handling a horse in a round pen. Rope skills, knowledge of the sort Elmer possessed, are a side of the picture too little taught by modern clinicians.

In this book, we'll explore some of the ways knots can make life easier and safer in handling horses. Instead of attempting to learn a vast quantity of them (*The Ashley Book of Knots* contains some four thousand!) we'll concentrate on some of the really useful ones, because over the years I've learned that we tend to retain only the ones we use. We'll learn to recognize a "good" knot—a knot that holds but can be untied after pressure—and we'll look into the world of hitches (systems for packing items onto a horse) and splices (useful ways of joining ropes and creating loops).

After that, it's a matter of practice, frequently tying the knots we've learned and looking for more ways to apply them.

And if messing with knots creates more excuses to mess around with our horses, so be it. It's all to the good!

# 1. THE SQUARE DEAL

Your first exposure to knots, to the need for tying a proper one, probably came when you struggled as a child with tying the laces on your shoes. What you were striving for, if you were properly taught, was a bow knot, which is merely a square knot tied with the top half-hitch made with two *bights* rather than two ends. Whoa! Bights?

So, a couple of simple definitions are in order. Walk over to a coil of rope and pick

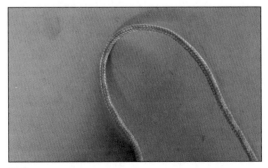

*Bight.*

up one end with your left hand. The part to your right, still in the coil or strung out somewhere, is called the *standing* part. The end in your left hand is, simply, the *end*. Make a loop or curve in the rope between the end and the coil and you have what's called a bight. Yes, *loop* works, too, and we'll use both terms.

## Rope Varieties

But before we get seriously into this business of knots, we need to look at just what sort of material we're using to make them, namely the rope itself. Go to a big hardware store and have a look at what's available. There are colored ropes, drab ropes, twisted ropes, woven ropes—the variety seems endless.

For purposes of this book, and in my own use as a horseman, I incline toward three-strand twisted ropes. Normally, these have been twisted clockwise, with what's called a right-handed "lay," but that's not always true. Because clockwise is the usual direction, rope coils well in the same direction, clockwise. As a left-hander, I sometimes used to go in the opposite direction, and it did not work very well. Finally, I figured out the problem.

Yes, there are ropes twisted the other direction, such as lariat ropes especially built for left-handed ropers. However, off-the-shelf twisted ropes will normally be of right-handed lay, and the only reason that's very relevant to us is in coiling the rope.

Many useful ropes come braided, and they're often easy on the hands and attractive in appearance. However, my preference for three-strand twisted rope comes from the ease with which I can splice it. Tying eye splices in twisted rope is relatively simple. Yes, braided rope can be spliced as well, but the procedure is somewhat more complicated, and it requires a few tools and accessories (fids and pushers) that match the particular rope. In a backcountry camp, you're not likely to have the correct accessories on hand. Splicing three-strand twisted rope requires no tools.

## Rope Materials

As to rope materials, all fall under two categories, natural or artificial. Natural fiber ropes are made of nature's own materials, grown by humans as agricultural products. Hemp, manila, sisal, and cotton, among other organic fibers, have been used to make rope. During the era of sailing ships, hemp and manila were major crops because a single large sailing ship could require several miles of rope for its rigging.

Natural fiber ropes vary, of course, but they usually are somewhat rougher in texture than artificial fiber, which can be an advantage—they're less likely to slip through your hand—but also less comfortable to handle. All natural ropes are subject to rot and to absorbing water and becoming heavier and swelling because of it. Hemp ropes during the sailing era had to be tarred to prevent rot, a nasty job given to the lowest-ranked sailors.

When a natural rope absorbs water, its knots become more difficult to untie. Freezing also makes things tough. I've struggled to remove frozen cotton ropes from a highline early in the morning after a wet snow and then a freeze at high altitude. While I know purist packers who still insist on "grass ropes" and who like the natural friction when tying hitches, artificial ropes have pretty much taken over both on land and sea. If used, natural ropes must be cared for properly and dried and cleaned before storage.

Artificial ropes also come in a variety of materials, the three most common being nylon, polyester, and polypropylene, though Dacron rope is also highly valued on boats because of its low-stretch characteristics and resistance to sunlight degradation. Nylon is the strongest, but it also stretches a great deal—good in some ways and not in others. I don't care to use nylon for sling ropes on my packsaddles, because it seems you can never get a hitch truly tight—the line just keeps stretching.

Polypropylene is seldom used in the horse world, though I've seen hay nets and such made of it. If you're a water skier, you're familiar with it. Since ropes made of polypropylene float, they're handy in some nautical uses when the skipper must avoid using a rope that will sink and tangle in the boat's propeller. A ski rope of polypropylene stays visible on the water's surface, another plus.

Nearly all artificial ropes are more slippery to handle than natural ones—again, both an advantage and a disadvantage. They can also be manufactured in many colors, handy for sailors who can use one color for sheets, another for halyards, and so on. But I use this feature as a horseman, as well. My manty ropes are black with a red thread running through them, while my sling ropes are yellow.

Peruse my tack room and you'll likely see more polyester ropes than those of any other substance. All are three-strand twisted types. Nearly as strong as nylon, polyester doesn't stretch as much, is abrasion resistant, and is nice on the hands. Some I've purchased is excessively slippery, but this characteristic seems to fade a bit when the rope becomes well worn. One criticism I hear of all "poly" rope, however, is that when used for picket lines the stuff can give a nasty rope burn if rubbed quickly across a pastern or leg. However, it's not alone in this respect. On a recent trip a mule pulled a cotton rope through my grip, and it, too, gave me a nasty burn.

## Square Knot

Ropes of many types are our materials, and knots are tools for using them well. And one of the most fundamental knots, the *square knot*, is the place where we start and also the basis for the knot with which we tie our shoes. Although sometimes considered a knot for joining two rope ends of the same diameter, there are better knots than the square knot for that purpose. Even though the two ropes may be of the same diameter, one may be of a stiffer material, and the knot may fail. Thus, the square knot isn't the best one for escape from a burning building by tying pieces of various materials together—there would be better knots for such an emergency (and also considerably worse ones). Still, the square knot is relatively strong as long as it joins identical diameters and types of rope, and it's relatively easy to untie after it's been pressured, a major consideration with all knots. Its best use is to secure a line around an object such as a post, for tying a bucket to a corral rail or your jacket behind the cantle of your saddle on a trail ride.

At sea, the square knot is called the reef knot, because when shortening sail, loops of rope ("line," at sea) are tied around the gathered material at the bottom of the sail to make it smaller when the breeze becomes a wind and the sea turns choppy. The loop of rope going around the gathered portion of the sail has been traditionally tied with a square (reef) knot.

On land, the hay bales you feed your horse came from a machine that holds spools of twine. The person running the machinery ties the twine at the end of one spool to the beginning of the next with, usually, a square knot, since it's neat and smooth enough to go through the knotting devices on the baler.

In this case, with twine that's identical in size, brand, and texture, the knot holds quite well. However, before trusting the knot, the operator gives both the standing portions and the end portions of the twine a good strong pull to tighten the knot, and he trims the ends close to smooth the knot for pulling through the machine.

Like many "good" knots, the square knot simply looks right when tied. Pass one strand over and under the other, then bring the ends

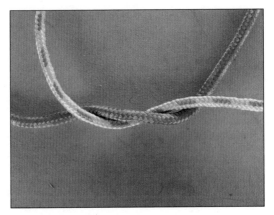

*Square knot, step 1.*

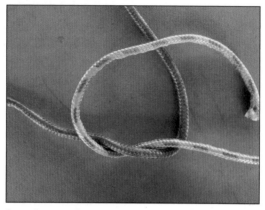

*Square knot, step 2.*

up, and going the other direction, again pass the same strand under and over the other.

Then pull both strands on each side tight. The knot looks nice and symmetrical, appearing as a loop catching another loop. After pressure the knot can still be untied, though sometimes with effort, meeting that other crucial qualification of a "good" knot.

## Granny Knot

Do it wrong, going opposite with the second hitch, and you get a useless knot with an

*A finished square knot.*

insulting name, the "*granny knot.*" Note that on the granny knot the two strands coming out of each side of the knot do not come out together—one is over the loop strand, one under. This knot will not hold, and if it does, pressure will leave it virtually impossible to untie. A sailor probably named it in contempt of all landlubber things ("Looks like a knot my granny would tie"), forgetting that his grandmother in those times with her knitting, sewing, and other skills probably knew as many knots as he did.

*A granny knot.*

## Square Knot with Slip Loop

Working on various ranches, when ropes, horses, and livestock dominate everyday life, the most common knot I have used has been a square knot with a slip loop. This variation is handy for tying a rope around an object, making for a quicker release. Start with the first half of a regular square knot. Then, on the top half, create a bight (loop) to wrap, rather than a single end. Unless significant pressure has been put on the knot, it's quick to untie

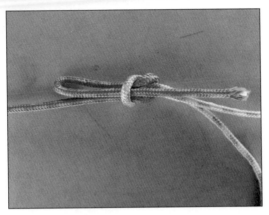

*A square knot with a slip loop.*

by pulling the end of the slip loop. Since at sea "shaking out a reef," or freeing the sail for more area and speed, had to be done quickly, this knot is also known as the "*slipped reef knot*," because it can be untied quickly.

## Bow Knot

Now, back to tying your shoes. You learned this knot as a youngster, but if your shoes perpetually seem to untie themselves, perhaps you didn't learn well. The *bow knot* is simply a square knot tied with two slipped loops instead of one. The knot begins the same way, but then you create two bights. Loop the two under and over as on the first half of the knot, and you have a bow knot. But if you go wrong on the top half you have a granny knot with two loops. This knot is harder to untie and less reliable.

## Half Hitch

Backing up, the simple knot you tied as the first half of the square knot was actually a *half knot*, though it's also referred to as a *half hitch*. Pull on the longer, standing portion, and push the knot down against the object you're securing, and the half knot forms. Put a different way, the working end of your rope is brought over and under the standing part, and the load pulls on the standing part.

In many respects, the half hitch is an ingredient knot, making up part of many knots and hitches but having little strength of its own before anything is added. I do, however, often

*Two half hitches: a handy way to hang a bucket.*

use a slightly stronger version of the half hitch
that's quick to tie and quick to release. It consists simply of a single half hitch tied with the
end of the rope doubled. You can tie it in an
instant with one hand. I use this as the prelim-
inary knot for a basket hitch during packing
when I've put the manty in place and need to
hold it and its mate on the other side briefly
while I check to see that the packs balance.
(We'll delve deeper into this procedure in
chapter 4.)

There's another common use for the half hitch that becomes, with the help of a loop, extremely strong. The very popular rope halters many of us use are secured by a simple half hitch. How can this incomplete knot be strong enough to take a hard pull when a thousand-pound horse takes issue with being tied up? The secret is that the half hitch is tied *through and around* a loop built into the halter. When pressured, the half hitch jams into that loop, tightening upon itself. Lead ropes are

*A properly tied halter.*

sometimes secured the same way to another loop built into rope halters lying under the jaw of the horse.

But many people make the mistake of tying the half hitch above, rather than below the halter loop. Now the strength is gone, because pressure tends to pull the half hitch away from the loop, rather than jamming into it. Such a tie relies totally upon the half hitch for strength. Tie a rope halter in this fashion and you may find your horse grazing

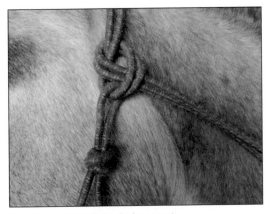

*In an improperly tied halter the knot may jam.*

in the next pasture (which in the West can be miles away). Or, once pressure has been applied, the knot may jam in such a way you have trouble removing the halter.

## Sheet Bend

There's another reason this halter knot is so strong. The half hitch tied correctly in conjunction with the halter loop is, in fact, another very popular and useful knot, the *sheet bend*. If you've been tying your halter in this correct manner, you've only had to tie the half hitch because the loop is already built into the halter. But the two combined create a sheet bend.

The name of the sheet bend, like those of many other knots, is nautical. Anyone but the most inveterate landlubber knows that the sheets on a sailboat are not the sails, but the lines (ropes) that control the angle of the sails. A drunken sailor might be "three sheets to the wind"—the alcohol has taken over. He's given up control and just let the sheets go.

The word "bend," as a noun, has as one of its more obscure meanings (according to Merriam-Webster), "a knot by which one rope is fastened to another or to some object." The sheet bend is an excellent knot for either purpose, and it's a better one for tying two ropes together than the square knot. Unlike the square knot, the sheet bend is secure even when the two ropes joined are of different diameters.

The sheet bend is simple to tie. Step 1: Make a loop (bight) in the end of one rope. If the ropes are of unequal size, make the bight in

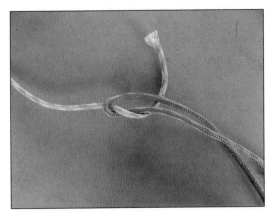

*Sheet bend, step 1.*

the larger one. Then bring the other rope through the loop from below, around the loop, under itself, and out.

Step 2: Tie it so that the free ends of both ropes emerge on the same side. Pull it tight. This knot is very strong, yet relatively easy to untie after pressure is applied. In many respects, it resembles the bowline, which we'll study in the next chapter. I find myself using the sheet bend frequently now that I've learned it, wondering why I didn't catch on to it much earlier in life.

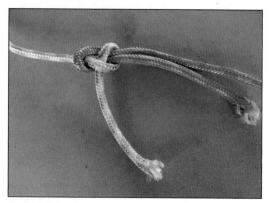

*Sheet bend, step 2.*

## Rope Buckle

The *rope buckle* is a simple variation of the sheet bend, used with an eye splice. It's the same knot you use in attaching a rope halter and is quick and easy to detach and adjust. A useful variation is to make it *quick-release* by inserting a bight rather than the end of the rope below the rope where it initially emerges through the eye splice. Unless extreme pressure has been applied a quick yank releases the buckle.

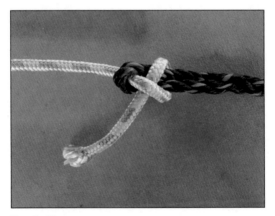

*Rope buckle.*

## Clove Hitch

Two knots that are very useful in the equine world involve tying two half hitches. The *clove hitch* can be used anywhere you want to secure the center of a rope against pull in both directions. For instance, you can tie the center of a line to your saddle horn, then structure various hitches for holding packs on a horse. (We'll practice that in chapter 4.) One way to think of the clove hitch is as two half hitches that go in opposite directions, usually tied around a pole or post.

To tie a clove hitch, (step 1) make a loop in the rope, then another identical one. Place the two together (step 2), one over the other.

Or, as the illustrations show (and this might be easier), tie it around a post or saddle horn. Wrap the rope under the post or rail, bring it around to the left of the standing part, then back over the rail and back under itself so that it heads in the opposite direction. The lanyard on my Marine officer's sword is tied this way, probably because the strap (made up of two strands) proceeds in two directions,

*Clove hitch, step 1.*

*Clove hitch, step 2.*

*Clove hitch on a saddle horn.*

one part up toward the base of the handle, the other hanging down toward the blade of the sword.

## Lanyard Hitch

However, the other similar knot we'll examine is the one often called the "*lanyard knot,*" and it looks neat when used for hanging a bucket from a corral rail (or a watch fob attached to a ring or belt). My other frequent use of this knot, which is simply two facing half hitches, was taught me on an elk hunt by my wife's older cousin George, a fine horseman. Bucking wet snow up to the knees of my tall horse, we'd followed tracks of a herd of elk that eventually had dived into a patch of deep, dark timber. We were sure that if we tracked them farther, they'd simply emerge on the other side, out of view.

We hitched on a simple plan. I'd lead George's horse around the timber and down the mountain to a clearing we knew to be at the base of the hillside at the edge of the timber patch; he would hunt his way down through the woods. With luck, one of us would "get into elk" and acquire some fine winter meat.

I tied the reins of George's horse in some haphazard manner to his saddle horn, intending to lead the horse down by its lead rope, but George said, "No, tie the reins up with two half hitches." I must not have responded immediately, so he explained, "Take both reins up on one side of his neck and tie them to the horn with two half hitches."

What he'd asked finally sank in, and with his help I tied the reins up the way I've always done since, both reins on one side of the neck (step 1), the two half hitches tied so the reins emerge neatly together, as shown (step 2).

I've found this to be the best method for tying reins up if a horse must be led; it's secure and neat, and the reins stay in place quite well even when leading the horse through brushy areas.

*Tying reins to horn with lanyard hitch (two half hitches), step 1.*

*Lanyard hitch, step 2.*

*Reins secured with two half hitches.*

## Latigo Knot

Another common use of two facing half hitches on saddles is what we often call a "*latigo knot*." Originally, the knot was the universal way of tightening the cinch (girth) on a western saddle. This need has been largely replaced today by cinches with tongues to buckle, but it's still in use, particularly on packsaddles. It's a good one for tightening cinches, because you simply pull up on the latigo where it protrudes through the cinch

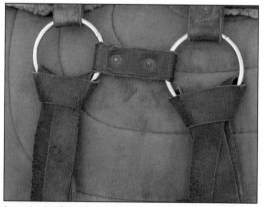

*Latigo hitches for cinches, also known as lanyard knots, or two facing half hitches.*

ring, pull the slack into the loop on the face of
the knot, then pull the bitter end of the latigo
tight, closing the loop. The latigo knot, made
up of two facing half hitches, looks good, lies
relatively flat under the stirrup leathers or
pack horse load, and holds well.

## Dragging with Half Hitches

Separate half hitches can also be used in a
series to tighten a line around a bunch of loose
objects, cinching them together. This is how a
manty is tied for packing (see chapter 4), but
the method is useful in many other ways as
well. Again, my first exposure to this approach
involved a mentor, this time my father-in-law
Elmer. I was helping him irrigate an alfalfa field.
Since there was no way to use the Jeep without crossing the flooded field and making ruts,
he always used his saddle horse Brownie to
move the dam materials to the next "set," the
next place we needed to dam up the ditch to
flood another increment of the field.

The dam materials were a pretty considerable bundle, consisting of a strong pole

perhaps twelve feet long, ten to fifteen two-by-six boards of various lengths, and a canvas tarp around sixteen feet long and eight feet wide. We pulled the dam out, letting the backed-up water flow down the ditch. Elmer folded the wet canvas carefully, and slapped it in place behind the cantle of his saddle, where he tied it with the saddle strings. Brownie, well trained for this procedure, hardly flinched when the cold, wet tarp was draped over him, but waited patiently for his next task.

Elmer then laid a loop from a well-worn lariat out on the ground (he reserved his "good" lariat for other purposes), and we stacked the boards and pole carefully so that their ends projected into the loop. When the boards were neatly stacked, Elmer tightened the loop. Then he worked the lariat rope around the big bundle with several loops, each half-hitched as shown. I found it hard to believe that this loose bundle of heavy boards would stay together while dragged over the ground, but he assured me it would.

*Dragging with a loop and half hitches.*

Elmer tightened Brownie's cinch and told me, "When you do this, when you cinch him this tight, make sure you loosen it a notch again after the pull." Elmer mounted up, and I handed him the rope. He carefully took two "dallies" (wraps) around the saddle horn, warning me that when doing this you're always to keep your thumb in the air, never turning your hand downward. "Too many ropers," he said, "are missing a thumb!"

I watched as he eased Brownie forward, taking the slack out of the rope, then as Brownie arched his neck and lowered his body into the pull. The rope tightened, and then each half hitch tightened as well, compressing the bundle into a neat package, finally beginning to move. Then Brownie dragged it the needed fifty yards without a single wet board escaping the pile. The series of half hitches had worked in concert to compress the load and keep it together. I was impressed.

This method is an excellent one for dragging firewood logs to camp or a group of corral poles to a work site. I've used it behind a Belgian work horse to drag several small logs, trimmed of branches, out of the woods together. You can use it on a single pole to teach your horse to drag, one of the handiest skills he can learn for backcountry use. He experiences the rope against his hip, the sensation of pull from the horn, the rearward view of an object moving mysteriously behind him. Perhaps the rope at some point gathers under his tail. When he's comfortable with all this he's likely to be ready to pony a pack horse.

## Rolling Hitch

Although I've haven't seen it used frequently in the horse world, the *rolling hitch* is one worth knowing. It somewhat resembles the clove hitch, but its purpose is different. The rolling hitch allows attachment to another rope or to a pole and is strong when the pull is in line with the point of attachment, rather than perpendicular to it. So, if you wanted to supplement the pull of one rope with another, the rolling hitch would work well, and it, too, could

*Rolling hitch, step 1.*

*Rolling hitch, step 2.*

be used to drag a pole into camp. In such a use it is much more secure than a clove hitch.

Start by wrapping the line around the object, then doing it a second time, each time crossing over the standing line (step 1). These wraps should be in the direction of the intended pull. Finally, (step 2) wrap it a third time, but this time above the standing line (away from the direction of pull). Then, complete the knot with a half hitch by tucking the end under the last wrap. Pull it tight before applying pressure.

# 2. THE ESSENTIAL BOWLINE

Ask a seasoned packer or sailor which knot he or she would choose to retain should a brain injury delete all but one knot from memory, and he'd almost certainly choose the *bowline*. It's been called the queen of all knots, the knot that will never fail, the knot with which you'd trust your life should the occasion demand.

Why is the bowline so special? First, it does not fail. It doesn't come untied under pressure, even when shaken around, if it's been pulled tight. Equally important, it never slips. Tie a loop into a rope with a bowline, throw the loop over a stump, and no matter how hard you pull, the loop stays the same size. And, no matter the pressure you've put on it, you can always get it untied. You can loop a nylon rope around the axle of a truck stuck in the mud, pull it out with another vehicle, and still untie the rope without ruining it.

The bowline is the knot you'd want to tie around your own body in an emergency situation or around the chest of a horse bogged down in the mud before pulling it free, secure in the knowledge it wouldn't tighten up and strangle when the pull was applied. You could also tie the ends of two ropes together in the most secure possible way by making a loop with a bowline, then tying the other rope through that loop and securing it with a bowline also—not a compact setup, but a very strong one.

Should you have to tie a horse up with only a rope around its neck, as Elmer did with Rosie, the bowline is safe and secure. And should it be necessary to restrain a horse by tying up a foot (for medication, perhaps, or after an encounter with a porcupine), the method we prefer begins with a bowline, this time at the base of the neck.

## Tying a Bowline

The bowline exists to make a fixed loop at the end of a rope, a loop of any size you choose.

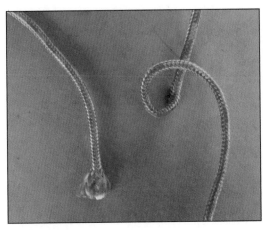

*Bowline, step 1.*

Usually it's tied as follows. Lay out the free end of your line using a twist to make a small loop (step 1).

Then bring the end of the line up through the hole (the rabbit comes out of the hole, step 2) and circle the standing part (the rabbit goes around the tree).

Then duck the end back down through the loop/"hole" (step 3).

Finally, pull the knot tight.

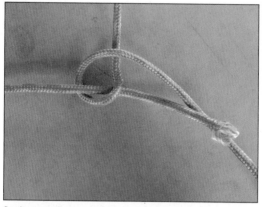

*Bowline, step 2.*

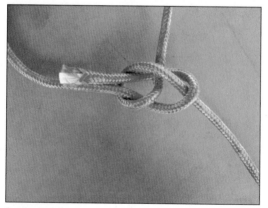

*Bowline, step 3.*

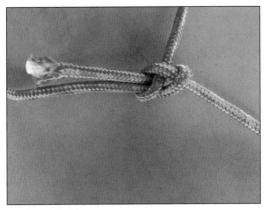

*Bowline, pulled tight.*

As a lefty, I tend to tie the bowline the opposite way, but the result is the same. I make the small loop in my right hand with the standing part on top, then bring the end down through the "hole," around the standing part, and back through the hole.

## Tying up a Horse with a Bowline

As a horseman one of my most common uses of the bowline has been to tie up the hind foot of a horse. Why and how do I do this? Let's back up. One of the safest things you can teach your horse is to freely give each of his feet, whether to a farrier or to a fence that happens to snag him. Teaching him to yield with his feet could prevent an injury or even save his life. Thus, I don't stop with halter-breaking our colts; I also teach them to lead by each foot, which is easier than it sounds. There's no need to pull hard on a given foot, but just exert a steady pressure. Annoyed at first, the colt soon figures out that he can release the pesky pressure by taking a step

*Teaching a horse to lead by each foot.*

toward you. When he's good at the first foot (one of his fronts) I proceed to the others. Usually each succeeding foot is easier.

Once this training is accomplished, hobbling becomes possible, then picketing on trips to the mountains with a hobble half on one front foot. But the time may come when the horse will have to be restrained, as mentioned above, to treat an injury or to pull porcupine quills. In any case, holding a foot up, even if the horse resists, is something the farrier will eventually require. Believing it best not to wait for an emergency, I teach our horses to accept restraint by tying up a hind foot as part of their training.

Tying up the foot begins with a piece of rope—around twenty feet is good—made of soft cotton if you intend to wrap it directly around his hind pastern. If you have a hobble half to use around the hind foot and intend to insert the rope through the ring, the texture of the rope is less important. But cotton is best for direct contact, because it's less abrasive and more comfortable for the horse.

*Attach hobble half on pastern.*

For safety, the colt should *not* be tied up to something secure during this procedure—it's far safer to have an assistant hold the lead rope. If you're alone, wrap the lead rope a turn or two around a post or pole rather than tying it, so that if the colt should spook during the process, the lead rope could allow slippage and prevent a fall.

Start with a bowline around the base of the horse's neck, right about where a horse collar fits on a draft horse (step 1).

*Tying up a foot, step 1: place a bowline around the neck.*

Then bring the rope down between the horse's hind legs (if you're going to wrap around the hind pastern) or through the ring of the hobble half (if you're using one). Then bring the rope back up along his side through the loop at the base of the horse's neck (step 2). This creates 2:1 leverage, and by pulling you can raise the colt's hind leg up under him.

However, I don't do that right away. Instead, I just take the slack out of the rope and tie it

*Tying up a foot, step 2.*

off with a half hitch with quick-release loop (see page 14). The colt may kick against the rope, testing it, but if you've trained him to lead by each foot he should accept the restraint readily. When he quits testing the rope, I'll untie the half hitch and pull the colt's foot slightly forward, holding on to the rope until he gets used to that. Finally, I'll raise it until it's just clear of the ground before tying it off.

Again, the colt may resist, kicking at the rope that restrains him, but soon he'll get used to it. The process will have increased his readiness to give a foot when asked, and you'll be confident that you could restrain his movement in an emergency. And you can have somewhat more confidence in his readiness to stand and wait for you, rather than hurt himself, should he be caught in barbed wire. The bowline is the only knot in which I have full confidence when tying the rope around the colt's neck, so it's the knot that makes the procedure possible.

## Running Bowline

Just as the bowline creates a fixed loop that will not tighten, another version of the same knot can do the opposite—produce a tightening loop you can throw around an object to snag it (perhaps as part of the procedure described for dragging poles in the last chapter) or as an impromptu lariat rope. The *running bowline* is a fine knot for this purpose. Why "running?" Again, the explanation is nautical. The word "running" when applied to knots and ropes means that a portion of the knot or hitch is designed to allow movement.

A sailing vessel has two kinds of rigging. *Standing* rigging holds the mast and spars in place. The standing rigging stays in a fixed position. *Running* rigging is made of lines (ropes) that run through various pulleys (blocks) to adjust the sails or other parts of the rig. The term "running" has stuck within the world of ropes and knots. It refers to a knot or hitch, part of which is made to move.

Tie a running bowline by making a large loop in the rope by going over, then under the standing portion (step 1). At the top of the large loop make another smaller one by twisting the rope (step 2).

Then, just tie a bowline by bringing the end of the rope up through the small loop (step 3), around the top of the large loop (the rabbit has come out of the hole and has gone around the tree), and now back down through the loop. Pull the knot tight (step 4).

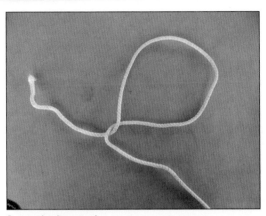

*Running bowline, step 1.*

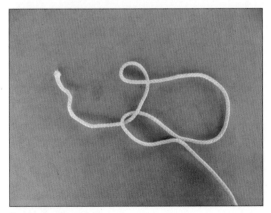

*Running bowline, step 2.*

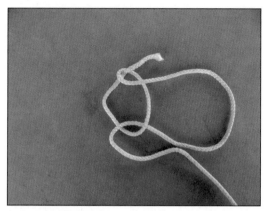

*Running bowline, step 3.*

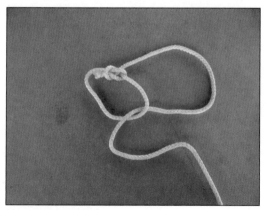

*Running bowline, step 4.*

The bowline is acting as the honda of your makeshift lariat. It has snagged the main part of the rope in such a way that it can "run," so you can make the loop as large as you wish, throw it around an object, and tighten it by a pull. No matter the pressure, you'll always be able to get the running bowline untied.

## Honda Knot

But if you only wish to create an impromptu lariat, the *honda knot* is more compact and very easy to tie. Knot guru Clifford Ashley wrote in *The Ashley Book of Knots* that he learned the honda knot from the famous cowboy author and illustrator Will James (whose cabin in the Pryor Mountains was located only fifty miles or so east of me as the crow flies).

To tie the honda knot, first tie an *overhand knot* in the end of your rope as a *stopper knot,* as shown, and pull it tight. The overhand knot is one you make frequently without think-ing; you simply make a loop in the rope and pass the end through it, then pull tight. It's probably the most-often used stopper knot,

*Overhand knot as stopper knot.*

defined as a knot in the end of a rope to make it easier to hold onto the end should it slip through your hand. Stopper knots are also used as a temporary way of keeping a rope from unraveling.

After you've made a tight overhand stopper knot, make a loose overhand knot eight or ten inches from the end of your rope (step 1).

Now bring that end up through one side of the overhead knot (step 2). Pull the loose knot tight, leaving a small loop to act as the honda (step 3).

*Honda knot, step 1.*

*Honda knot, step 2.*

*Honda knot, step 3.*

Now thread the other end of your rope through the loop to create the lariat.

Of course, it's extremely important never to place a lariat or other running loop around a horse's neck and then tie it to something solid. Traditional cowboys who roped horses from their remuda in a corral sometimes used a snubbing post, but only to wrap (dally) the lariat rope, not to tie fast. The rope was allowed to slip as necessary, much in the manner of the drag on a fishing reel. Also,

*Honda knot with end pulled through for lariat.*

the honda on the lariat was open enough that whenever slack was given in the lariat rope, the loop around the horse's neck also loosened. And, as the horses became used to the routine, they were in effect trained to be roped; when they felt the lariat around their necks, they gave to the pressure and avoided injuring themselves.

# 3. TRAIL KNOTS

Now it's time to get in the saddle, hit the trail, and use some of the knots we've discussed, perhaps learning a few more on the way. I emphasize the trail, because if you were the sort who only rides in an arena or on manicured bridle paths and has a groom (heaven forbid) to take care of all equine details for you, you would probably not be reading this book. Knowledge of knots is for the horseman or horsewoman who gets outside, goes places, and does things with his or her horse.

## Tying Your Horse
Let's start with some basics. Your horse, no matter how well trained, would be by choice a free-roaming creature, constantly searching for the most delicious bite of grass, ever aware of danger and ready to run should something suspicious present itself. Water a horse in a

creek and you'll notice that he rarely drinks his fill in one shot. Several times he'll raise his head quickly, look around, and then resume drinking. The waterhole is nature's ambush setup, where predators patiently wait, and your horse, no matter his thousand years of domestication, knows it.

Training changes all this, at least to a degree. But fundamental to your use of him is his willingness to stand tied, to comply with your wishes rather than with his instinct to run free. And for tying we need halters, lead ropes, and something solid to which to tie.

I emphasize "solid," because an ill-advised trend is now making the rounds involving "breakaway" systems for tying horses. The theory is that should a horse pull too hard it might hurt itself. So, at a certain point these breakaway halters or leads are designed to give way and allow the horse to leave the premises. One marketer of such systems hails from England, where, I suspect, a horse loose in a small paddock doesn't pose a huge problem. But traditionally, in the huge expanses of

American West, and even today, "being afoot" could actually cost you your life.

Bluntly put, whoever came up with this breakaway idea had never taken Psychology 101 and had never met a horse like Rosie (whose pull-back problem I discussed in the introduction). And he or she had certainly never had to walk five miles back to the home ranch because a saddle horse got away. A breakaway system will simply train your horse to pull back. The first time he frees himself may be an accident, a slight spook that results in a bit of a jerk, a release, followed by a taste of freedom (positive reinforcement). The next one will be deliberate—that grass tasted so good. From then on, he'll be a confirmed puller, to your distress and to his own peril. (Remember that busy highway or set of railroad tracks near your horse trailer?)

All young horses should be equipped with a stout halter, then halter trained in the hands of someone both strong and understanding. I don't halter train by pulling straight forward on the colt's head—that only encourages him to pull back against the pressure. Instead I stand to his side and simply take the slack out of the lead rope. He's uncomfortable with his nose restricted and moved slightly sideways, and sooner or later he figures out that he can make his own slack by easing toward me. I reward him verbally, and then take the slack out again. Soon he understands that comfort comes with compliance with the pressure, and he's halter broke.

Further, as described earlier, I teach the colt to give each foot, leading him by each in turn. When he's that far along, understanding he's to give to pressure either from the halter or from the foot, he should be tied up to something solid, tied up fairly high (no lower than natural nose level), and with a short rope (with perhaps three to four feet of lead). Tying high takes away the colt's leverage, tending to make his hind legs slip up under him. Always, though, I tie with a quick-release knot. Very few horses struggle very long, because it's uncomfortable for them. After a time or two they normally accept being tied up, and that's that.

*Tie high and fairly short for safety.*

## Types of Halters

A "breakaway" system, tying with weak reins rather than lead rope, or tying to something flimsy can "unlearn" ("extinguish" is the psychological term) this training. Also, early in training, a horse might spook and inadvertently break a weak halter or lead rope. If odds seem good this might happen, it's probably best to use the very strongest setup available, which is a halter and lead rope with no hardware whatsoever. The modern synthetic rope tied halters are incredibly strong. Add a strong lead rope either hitched to the loop on the halter with a half hitch on the pre-tied loop (which creates a sheet bend, as discussed on page 18) or attached via an eye splice, and you eliminate all metal snaps or buckles that could conceivably break.

Of these, I like using a lead rope with an eye splice best, because it's so easily removable. To attach, simply slip the eye splice through the halter loop, and then bring the end of the lead rope back through the eye splice, pulling the whole rope through. If you prefer to ride with the lead rope attached, this makes a nice, compact, and light attachment, without a metal snap to click along, annoying both you and your horse. Yet, it's easily removable. And, if you decide you prefer a snap, you can attach the snap to the eye splice the same way. (We'll discuss making lead ropes with eye splices and back splices in chapter 7, see page 164.)

Much as I recognize the superior strength of tied-type synthetic rope halters (and I use them a great deal), I actually prefer flat strap-type halters and lead ropes with strong snaps for riding. Here's why: Since tying with reins is taboo except in emergencies (the reins are weak, and a pull on the bit can hurt a horse's mouth), I tend to ride with the halter in place under the bridle. A flat halter so placed is more comfortable for the horse than a rope halter, with its knots and circular material.

The key is to buy high-quality halters. Very nice leather halters used to be common, and they're still available. Good ones are expensive, but it's true that there's probably nothing nicer for the horse against his skin than leather, the most natural material of all, and some are also padded or lined with soft latigo leather. But leather must be cared for, cleaned, and occasionally oiled, and most horsemen are a bit too impatient to care for gear properly.

Thus, nylon has largely replaced leather for halters in everyday use, but nylon halters aren't all the same. The very thin ones, often priced as low as ten bucks, are flimsy, and their hardware is extremely suspect. Spend a little more, and get halters of high quality. These will have relatively thick nylon or doubled strapping. The metal rings on them are likely to be of higher quality.

My reason for preferring lead ropes with swivel snaps rather than those with ropes attached semi-permanently (the factory knots pulled tight are hard to untie) stems from my work in the backcountry, where I'm likely to use a highline to restrain my horses. The horse's lead *must* have a swivel where it attaches to the highline, since the animal is free to move in a circular pattern under the highline. Lack of a swivel will mean a ruined rope by morning. Hardware highline loops with swivels are available, but in my experience a swivel on the lead rope itself is still necessary. If the horse circles contrary to the direction in which the rope was twisted as it was made, a rope without a swivel simply unravels. Other types of rope will twist into knots.

The snap should not be a weak sliding type made of brass. A "bull" snap is stronger, if less handy, assuming it's of high-quality construction. I've seen a few poorly made ones. As mentioned, a lead rope with a heavy snap at one end should not be left attached to the halter as you ride. The snap will annoy the horse and even affect his sensitivity to the neck rein. Coil the rope compactly and tie it to your saddle strings, making sure the string goes through the snap itself as part of the coil. Tie it off with a square knot.

## Tie-Up Knot

There are many ways to tie a horse up with his lead rope attached to something solid. For maximum security, you might use a bowline, and I've been known to do that in wilderness country when I need to leave my horse for a long period of time. However, the *tie-up knot* I normally use is an extremely simple one taught me by my wife and father-in-law. It's a type of slip knot, quick to tie and relatively quick to release, unless it has withstood extreme pressure.

Simply pass the lead rope around the post or tree and bring the end back toward you.

*Tie-up knot, step 1.*

*Tie-up knot, step 2.*

Twist to make a small loop with the standing portion on top (step 1). Place the loop on the other side of the span of rope between the horse and the post (step 2).

Now pass a loop (bight) through that small loop and pull the whole thing tight against the post (step 3). You now have a secure knot that can be untied with one jerk. However, it's easy to pass another loop through the first one and even do that several times, creating a chain you can untie with a series of jerks.

*Tie-up knot, step 3.*

*Tie-up knot, step 4: after pulling one or more bights through, put end through for safety.*

For maximum security, as a last step I put the end of the lead rope back through the final loop (step 4). When untying I'll need to remove that end from the loop before I start pulling to release.

## Rope Types on the Trail

Lead ropes come in all sorts of material, cotton, nylon, manila, and poly being the most common (see chapter 1, page 2). To review, cotton is nice on the hands, and for this reason I like to lead my packhorse with a cotton rope. However, cotton is relatively weak, so cotton lead ropes must be made with a larger diameter to compensate, which in turn makes them bulkier to knot. Another disadvantage comes in cold weather. In a fall hunting camp in the mountains, I've tied a horse with a wet cotton rope after a snowstorm, then tried hard to untie the horse the next morning after the temperature has plummeted. Cotton absorbs moisture, which then freezes when the temperature drops during the night.

Nylon is incredibly strong, and it comes in many configurations. As mentioned earlier, I tend to prefer three-strand twisted rope, no matter what the material, because it's so easy to splice. But some of the soft nylon braided ropes are very nice on the hands. Nylon stretches a great deal, a good thing for a lead rope since the stretch softens the jerk if a horse pulls back.

Of the several types of rope nicknamed "poly," it's polyester that I use most often for the sling ropes on my packsaddles, because I prefer less stretch for that purpose, and I prefer it for highlines for the same reason. A highline of nylon rope is certainly strong, but you'll find yourself constantly tightening it.

Manila can be nice on the hands, is relatively strong, and is easy to splice. Being of natural fiber, however, it's more susceptible to rot than most of the synthetics, and while it doesn't absorb moisture as readily as cotton, a wet manila lead rope is still heavier and less handy than a dry one.

## Trail Hazards

On the trail, unless you put all your gear on a pack animal, you'll take some (hopefully not too much) along on your saddle horse. But before we get to details about hauling gear on your saddle horse, a word about safety. All knowledgeable equestrians have an absolute phobia about becoming inadvertently "tied" to a horse. The nightmare most often emphasized is that of falling or being bucked off and catching one's foot in the stirrup.

Riding in Spain using English cavalry saddles, our guide "tested" us by ordering a canter (gallop, actually) up a gravel road the first time we mounted. I hadn't studied my saddle adequately, and while galloping I realized that my right foot was fixed in the too-small stirrup. I rode relatively well, so there was no real danger, but the mere thought of becoming hung up was enough to spoil my pleasure. At the first rest stop I was able to swap stirrups with a woman whose own were excessively large.

Tapaderos can help prevent that horrid scenario by blocking one's foot from slipping all the way through the stirrup. Proper footwear helps, too; a good heel on one's boot can prevent the foot from slipping too far forward. I avoid boots with an excessively aggressive traction tread, because they're more likely to become caught as you dismount. And, of course, a gentle, well-trained horse always increases one's odds of survival!

But there are many other possible pitfalls, things that could "glue" you to the horse, and they usually involve ropes or straps. Years ago, saddling up with my father-in-law, I noted that the latigo on my cinch was unnecessarily long, and I asked Elmer whether it should be trimmed off, because it hung nearly to the ground. "It's okay," Elmer said, "because it doesn't make a loop."

It took a while for that to sink in. The strap hanging straight down wasn't a hazard, in his opinion, because it wouldn't likely catch on anything. But if I'd tied it up in some haphazard fashion I might have created a loop that, in a "wreck," could catch my leg or my arm. That conversation has stuck with me. Any rope or strap that creates a loop is a potential hazard. These things include a lariat or lead rope too loosely coiled as it attaches to the saddle; a mecate stuck into your belt (a current fad pushed by some clinicians that is dangerous for the average trail rider); even one-piece (loop) reins, as opposed to split reins; all have potential to catch a leg or arm should your horse "blow up" because he meets a bear on the trail or a bicycle hurdling silently toward him down a mountain trail at thirty miles per hour.

## Pack Weight and Placement

Another potential hazard I see frequently are saddle packs behind the cantle piled high, bags that are too big, both to the detriment of the horse and to the possible chagrin of the rider should he or she catch a leg on the gear when dismounting. Huge-capacity saddle packs are pushed by some manufacturers to transport a full complement of camping gear on one's saddle horse along with the rider. The problem with these large packs is that people tend to find ways to fill them.

Besides the element of risk, we must consider the welfare of the horse. Horses carry weight most efficiently if it's near their center of gravity, which on most horses is fairly far forward, just back from the "elbow" of the front leg, and about a third of the way up their body. A heavy person rides with much of his or her weight behind that point. Add heavy packs behind the cantle of the saddle and you're probably stressing the horse's back and also interfering with his balance. That's a safety issue.

Another unwise trend I see today, especially among hunters, is that of a rider in the saddle carrying a heavy backpack on his back. The idea is for the rider to have all his essential gear with him when he steps off the horse and ties up to go look for a deer or elk. But such a pack creates several problems. Again, it puts weight too far back on the horse, and it raises the center of gravity on the horse's back. Should the horse need to go up an extremely steep incline, weight this high could conceivably pull him over backwards, a deadly scenario.

Here's my progression for tying on gear while I ride, from lightest to heaviest. For a day ride when it's not too hot (my Norwegian blood doesn't handle heat well), I just wear a light vest with many pockets. A small camera can go in one, a first aid kit in another, perhaps a sandwich in still another. A canteen or water bottle can be carried on the belt.

Nothing need be tied on the saddle either in front or in back.

Next up, when more gear is needed, I use pommel (horn) packs. Anything heavy—a bigger camera, water bottles, extra food, binoculars—goes in them. Slipping the bags onto the saddle horn isn't secure enough by itself, and they tend to bump my leg, so I also tie a saddle string securely around each with a square knot or a square knot with slipped loop. If your saddle has D-rings on the pommel, you can use cord to secure them. (The more saddle strings and D-rings on a trail saddle the better, and if your saddle has too few of each, have a saddle maker install more.) By keeping heavier items forward, I'm helping my horse by remembering his center of gravity.

## Quick-Attach/Quick-Release Knot

When more gear is needed and my small pommel bags won't hold everything, I'll still try to keep weight forward. Perhaps I'll buy a set of larger pommel bags—they do exist. Water bottles in sheaths made with a snap to

*Quick-release knot, step 1.*

*Quick-release knot, step 2.*

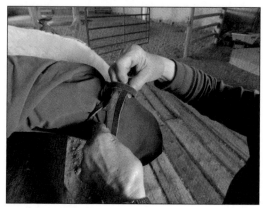

*Quick-release knot, step 3.*

go onto a D-ring can be carried outside the pommel bags. But a rain slicker or extra jacket probably needs to go behind the cantle. Roll it as compactly as possible and tie it tightly. I use a secure but quick-release method for tying objects with the saddle strings, learned from my wife and father-in-law. The method is simply a series of slipped half-knots. Emily starts by building the first half of a square knot (step 1) but pulling one strand as a loop (step 2), inserting a loop from the other side into the first one (step 3), and so on.

In each case after inserting the loop within a loop, she pulls on the opposite strand (step 4). The end result is a knot she can detach quickly by pulling on the strands with both hands, alternately. It's quicker and easier than it sounds.

Finally, now pushing the maximum weight and bulk I like to carry on my saddle horse, I'll reluctantly tie on saddle bags behind the cantle. I have a wonderful pair made of heavy leather by a good friend who imprinted our

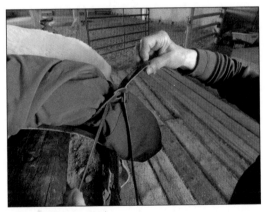

*Quick-release knot, step 4.*

livestock brand on them. They're extremely well made and durable. However, even empty, they're heavy. Nylon bags are less classy, but they're much lighter, and some come insulated so your lunch stays cool. And they're available in bright colors, a plus during hunting season or when riding in remote country where some sort of disaster could make your visibility an important rescue advantage. But don't buy the biggest saddle bags you can find; they'll only tempt you to take along more than you should.

## Securing Firearms

Much of backcountry horse use, and in the Rocky Mountain West particularly, is connected with hunting tradition and thus involves carrying a rifle or shotgun on a saddle horse. People tend toward strong opinions about the proper way of carrying a relatively awkward item and about how its scabbard should be tied on. Complications have increased as scabbards have grown larger to accommodate bulkier firearms with large scopes, bipods, and other accessories. Horseback in the mountains, I've seen all sorts of variations.

First, it goes without saying that no firearm should ever be carried horseback with a cartridge in the chamber. Check, re-check, and then check again that the chamber is empty before sliding a rifle into a scabbard. The most common position seems to be butt forward and muzzle down at about 45 degrees, the scabbard riding under the stirrup leathers. This position is easier on the knee than a straight horizontal attachment, though one experienced mountain hunter I know carries

*Rifle scabbard in typical position.*

it that way, horizontally right under his knee. But then, he's tough as nails and probably doesn't even notice. My knee would complain.

The straps that come with saddle scabbards are often too short to use properly. If you're lucky, and they're of adequate length, the front one (toward the butt end of the rifle) can extend up through the gullet on the pommel of the saddle, and the rear can reach a D-ring (if your saddle has such) behind the cantle. Too often the rear strap won't be long enough, however, and you'll need to extend a pair of saddle strings down to meet a loop on the strap. I'd recommend tying the strings with a sheet bend.

I'll reiterate that if your saddle has no D-rings and/or stingy, short saddle strings, have a saddle maker fix the problem. I like saddle strings to be around two feet long and made of good, stout leather thongs.

## What Weight Can Your Horse Safely Bear?

When travelling horseback with gear, there comes a time when you have to question whether it's practical and humane to ask your saddle horse to carry you and perhaps an entire complement of even the lightest camping equipment. Yes, it's possible to assemble a bare-bones set of overnight necessities and get it all on your saddle horse along with your saddle and your own body, packing it neatly with proper knots. But unless you weigh little more than a jockey and you're tough enough to get along with extremely Spartan gear, it's probably time to add a pack animal. We'll help with that in the next chapter. Meanwhile, a word about your saddle animal's weight-carrying ability is in order.

How much weight can your horse safely carry? There's no easy answer. The formula used by some riding stables—20 percent of the animal's weight—is useless if not downright damaging. There are simply too many variables. Can an overweight fourteen-hundred-pound horse really carry more weight than the same horse, slimmed and conditioned to twelve hundred pounds?

Indeed, as horses (and other four-legged animals) grow larger, their efficiency tends to diminish. A Percheron is able to carry more than a Welsh pony, true, but he can probably carry a *smaller percentage* of his body weight, because he must support his own very heavy body.

Further, the conformation of a horse has much to do with weight-carrying ability. Smallish Icelandic horses routinely carry large people and do so at a fast clip. Among their other assets are very broad loins. You can feel a horse's loin muscle by pressing firmly on his back behind the rib cage and dragging your hand down one side of his torso or the other. At some point, you'll feel a drop-off—that's the end of the muscle. For weight carrying, the further the loin muscle extends down to the side, the better.

Good bone is also an asset for carrying heavy weight, as is a short back. Dr. Deb Bennett, an expert on horse skeletal structure at the Equine Studies Institute, believes that the circumference of the front cannon bone on a saddle horse should measure a minimum of seven inches per thousand pounds of weight.

Maturity, which doesn't come until age six, is a necessity for carrying heavy weights over a sustained period of time. Placement of weight on the horse, as we've discussed, is important, and so is the ability of the rider. The person who sits like a sack of potatoes, who moves little with the horse, makes it tough for the animal, while the good rider unconsciously helps the horse.

One conformational asset in horses, which helps with mounting and balancing gear on both saddle and pack horses, is prominent withers (the high point, just in front of the saddle). A horse with good withers holds the saddle better than one with a sausage-shaped back. But that's not an excuse to tie gear on in a sloppy or unbalanced fashion. If your saddle continues to list in one direction, and you believe you're riding in a balanced, square fashion, move a piece of gear from the listing side to the other side. Sometimes it doesn't take much: something no heavier than a water bottle can do the trick.

## Tying to the Saddle

One area where we actually want to *avoid* tying a knot is when we pony another horse, perhaps a pack animal, or drag something with our mount. Never tie fast to the saddle horn or another part of the saddle. Yes, there was a tradition in the roping world among true cowboys, particularly those in Mexican and South American tradition, that involved tying the end of the lariat rope fast to the saddle horn, but few, if any of us, are of the level of horsemanship (with horses at the level of training) necessary to prevent disaster with that approach.

That said, utilizing your horse's strength and size, as Elmer did in moving irrigation boards, can be useful in a host of ways. With a well-trained horse, you can drag firewood into camp or in an emergency pull an animal out of a bog (an advanced skill I hope you never need). The trick is to handle ropes and knots with safety in mind, since the power of a horse hitched to a rope that somehow inadvertently wraps around you means serious consequences indeed.

Teach your horse to pull by dragging a loose rope first, then perhaps a tire, around the arena. Assuming you ride with a western saddle, instead of tying any sort of knot, take a dally (wrap) around the horn with your free hand, thumb in the air. (Like all good "using" horses, your horse should neck rein. If he isn't so trained, that's another task to be accomplished.)

Steer ropers consider three full wraps around the horn to be the minimum required to hold the pressure of an animal at the end of a lariat rope. But use just one wrap when first instructing your horse by dragging the rope or a very light object. If your saddle horn is slippery, you can add a "dally wrap," purchased from a western tack shop, to create friction, or approximate one by cutting across a car or truck inner tube. Cut a swath about an inch wide, which creates a loop, then place it over the saddle horn, twist, go over again, and so on until your horn is tightly sheathed in rubber.

## Timber Hitch

One of the handiest ways to attach your rope to an object, such as a log you wish to drag into camp for firewood, is the *timber hitch*; it's so simple that at first glance you might be surprised it works. Just place your rope around the object, bring the free end around the standing part, and then coil it several times around itself to create something that looks vaguely like a hangman's knot. Pull out all slack so that the hitch lies tightly against

*Timber hitch.*

the log. You've now created a tightening loop around the log, similar in appearance to a lariat looped around the log, but requiring no other knot. The secret to its holding power is pressure. As the rope tightens the coil presses tightly against the log. It works well and is quick and easy to undo when the task is accomplished.

A properly packed saddle horse is one that appears neatly "dressed." Nothing protrudes in an ugly or hazardous fashion. No great bundle exists behind the cantle of the saddle to catch a foot when mounting or dismounting or to overload a horse where it damages his center of gravity or his spine. Pommel packs carry most of the heavy items. And, when too much gear is required, likely to happen on extended trips, on cold-weather trips (because of extra clothing), and on adventures that require hunting, fishing, or photography equipment, we turn to the pack animal (and the next chapter).

Adding a pack animal to your riding group, even on day rides, can relieve several riders of all the excess gear they'd normally take on their saddle horses, their lunches, extra jackets, water, and fishing poles, without even coming close to a pack animal's capacity. More riding groups should consider it.

# 4. PACKHORSE KNOTS

Expert horse and mule packers rival traditional sailors in their knowledge of knots and their many uses. A thorough knowledge of the various knots, hitches, and slings, including the diamond hitch and its many variations, can require a lifelong study. Among my packing acquaintances, however, most seem to have settled on a system that suits them and that answers their various needs, with further expertise interesting but not required. I've gone that same direction.

## No-Knot Pack Systems

Of course, you can begin packing without using knots at all! Packing systems are marketed which use the absence of knots as a selling point, perhaps tapping into the modern penchant for instant gratification. It's much easier in some folks' eyes if no learning is required.

There's nothing wrong with such systems. Usually they consist of a couple of soft panniers (bags that hang on each side of the animal) with web loops that attach over the crossed wooden slats of a sawbuck packsaddle or through the D-rings that form the top frame of a Decker saddle (more on these in a bit). A strap with buckle attaches under the belly of the pack animal to keep the panniers from flopping around. Then, buckles attach a top pack to the two panniers.

Use a little common sense, keep softer items next to the horse, harder items away from him, match the two panniers in weight, and you can hit the trail, assuming your pack animal has been trained to carry inanimate weight, and he's used to the breeching under his tail. But like most easy things in life, such a system has its limitations. First, it allows packing only what fits conveniently into the panniers. Second, in an emergency, such as a packhorse falling or becoming bogged down, it may be nearly impossible to release the load and save the animal without cutting straps, an action that will leave the system very hard to use after the crisis is over.

With systems using ropes and knots, you can use quick-release knots (which sometimes aren't all that easy to release after extreme pressure) or other knots and a sharp knife for such an emergency. If you must cut a rope, you can splice it or replace it with an extra picket rope from your packs and be on your way. And, since several packing systems don't require more than a few easily-learned knots, learning more about the art and science of packing, rather than taking the easiest route, will be well worth the trouble (and a good share of the fun).

## Saddle Panniers

But first, a word about the several systems available. The simplest is to use saddle panniers over a regular riding saddle you may already own as an extra. These consist of two cloth or plastic bags connected together with a top panel of material with cut-outs, a smaller one to slip over the pommel of the

*Riding saddle with saddle panniers.*

saddle, and a larger slit to go over the cantle. Saddle panniers normally have lids to close off the tops of the bags, though some of them, primarily intended for hunters who wish to pack out deer or elk quarters, may have only straps. Another strap with buckle goes under the horse's belly. The better saddle packs also have straps that go across the top of the bags joining the two to compress the load and hold it closer to the horse.

Saddle panniers work, but they're an expedient, often carried rolled up behind the cantle on the saddles of hopeful hunters. The hunter's intent, should he or she score on meat for the winter freezer, is to pack quarters in the panniers, leading the saddle horse to the trailhead. Removing the stirrups and placing them in the panniers is a good idea—otherwise they bump the horse under the load. Also, to better protect the horse, it's best to use an oversized packing pad under the saddle to extend farther down along the horse's flanks.

But I have found that even if saddle panniers are packed evenly, they don't stay in place all that well. The slits that go over the riding saddle have too much play in them, allowing too much side to side movement. We've installed grommets in the center of the front opening, where it goes over the horn and pommel, then tied a cord through the grommet and around the horn with a square knot, which helps. But usually we've ended up using a *basket hitch* to further support the panniers and keep them higher and tighter on the horse's back. This can be accomplished with some riding saddles, but the sling ropes would have to be brought along with the rider. We'll explore the basket hitch shortly.

Also, since the two bags are connected together by the top panel, they're almost impossible to lift onto the animal if they're fully loaded. The only alternative is to put the panniers on the saddle and load items into them when they're in position—a bit awkward if the horse is tall. If the horse is spooky, he may take issue with the appearance and smell of some of the items you place there, and you must constantly go from one of his sides to the other to keep things balanced. Getting an actual weight on each side with a packer's scale is virtually impossible, so you'll have to watch how the panniers ride and be quick to switch items to the other side if one pack begins to sink lower than its mate.

Unloading saddle panniers must be approached the same way and can be more than inconvenient. On a solo moose hunt many years ago, I had along an extra horse and a set of saddle panniers, this time attached to

*Sawbuck packsaddle with soft panniers.*

a sawbuck packsaddle. I was able to lift the front quarter of a young bull moose into each of the panniers while they were in place on Sugar, a moderately-sized gelding. The quarters weighed perhaps one hundred pounds each; I probably couldn't repeat this today.

All went well until I arrived in camp, exhausted from an afternoon that involved skinning and quartering such a large animal by myself in place on the ground. I found it utterly impossible to stand on my tiptoes, reach down into the panniers, and extract the heavy quarters. Had the panniers been conventional, separate ones, I could have removed them, but the top panel connecting the two saddle panniers made that impossible. I had no choice but to carefully remove breeching and breast collar, then checking and double checking to see that nothing would hang up, I removed the main cinch on the packsaddle and rolled the entire affair off Sugar's back. He was a good, steady horse and did not spook.

Another limitation of saddle panniers used on a riding saddle is their lack of a breeching (often "britchin'") to help the horse hold back the load on downhill grades. A crupper serves in this regard as well. With all packing, it's important to understand that the horse is carrying dead weight. The packs do not compensate for the horse's motion in the way a good rider does, which is why it's wise to limit total loads to around one hundred fifty pounds. A breeching or crupper helps stabilize the load on downhill grades. Either can be purchased separately and added to a riding saddle intended for packing use, but appropriate D-rings might have to be added to the extra saddle, and perhaps it's better to invest that money in an actual packsaddle.

## Sawbuck Saddle

The most economical of these is the time-proven sawbuck, also called the crossbuck. Its names derive from what used to be a common backyard fixture, a setup with crossed poles on which you could lay logs to saw into blocks for firewood. The sawbuck saddle has been a staple of packing in America for well over a century, and it's found in many parts of the world. On a riding trek in the mountains of southern Spain I saw packers using sawbuck saddles.

The sawbuck is made of two wooden "bars," shaped to fit the backs of most animals (though these can be custom shaped with a rasp if necessary). These are secured

*Mule with sawbuck packsaddle.*

together by two pairs of hardwood slats, fastened where they cross forming two Xs. Normally sawbucks are "double rigged," having two cinches rather than one, usually fastened with latigo knots (two facing half hitches), and they're equipped with a simple breast strap and the essential breeching.

The sawbuck works well for both the entry-level packer and the seasoned professional. The expert usually slings panniers or boxes on each side of the saddle and adds a top pack covered with a tarp, and finally secures everything with a variation of the diamond hitch attached to an extra cinch going under the animal's belly. Most of the various versions of the diamond hitch require a helper and considerable expertise, but they're worth exploring and most easily taught by a mentor who can walk you through the various steps.

The entry-level packer can acquire a sawbuck and equip it with soft panniers without a substantial investment. Simply load the panniers to be equal in weight (within five pounds or so of each other), keeping soft items such as sleeping bags and extra clothing next to the horse. Loop the straps over the two Xs of the sawbuck, fasten a strap underneath, and you're good to go. Top packs and the knots for securing them can be learned later (or you can use the buckle system if your panniers are made for it).

## Decker Saddle

The Decker saddle was developed in the mining areas of northwest Montana and northern Idaho, where awkward pieces of mining equipment and bags of ore had to be packed over mountain terrain. It's a very strong saddle, more likely to survive the fall of a pack horse. The Decker is a bit more expensive and a bit more versatile than the sawbuck, but well worth considering. Packing tends to be addictive—you'll probably want to expand your knowledge and capabilities.

Like the sawbuck, the Decker has two wooden bars that lie on each side of the horse's back parallel to the spine. These are fastened with iron D-rings rather than wooden slats and project upward in place of the two Xs of the sawbuck. Hitch ropes slide easily through these rings, an advantage.

The biggest single advantage of the Decker is the way it protects the horse from odd-shaped or hard-surfaced loads. Draped over the saddle, with the D-rings protruding through, is a large square of canvas or nylon called a "half-breed," stuffed with horsehair or foam. Installed horizontally on each side is a slim wooden board. The board, the padding in the half-breed, and the pack pad under the saddle all serve to protect the horse from

*Packing bridge planks on a Decker saddle.*

the pressure of an angular load. Now that many wilderness areas require bear-proof panniers—hard boxes made of metal or plastic—the Decker is increasingly the pack-saddle of choice.

However, the Decker works as well as the sawbuck for the entry-level packer who only wishes to hang on a couple of panniers. To avoid having to open the top straps each time the bags are put into place, purchase Decker hooks and install them in the straps, adjusting so that the tops of the panniers ride evenly. Then it's simply a matter of hooking the panniers to the saddle when you load up. But don't forget that essential belly strap to hold the panniers down and close to the horse. Since it always seems to loosen during the first mile, tighten it at your first rest stop.

## Basket Hitch

Soon you'll wish to move beyond the limitations of the most basic packing. Of the many hitches you can use, the basket hitch is one of the simplest and most versatile. It can be used with a sawbuck, a Decker, and some riding saddles to secure mantied loads, hard or soft panniers, or even two similar backpacks should you wish to give a couple of hikers a running start on their trek. And, it can supplement the belly strap connecting panniers as described above by further securing and steadying the load.

The iron rings of the Decker packsaddle make it especially handy for the basket hitch, because they reduce friction when pulling the hitch tight. The sling ropes on my Deckers are made of half-inch polyester rope, eye-spliced to the D-ring on my left as I face the horse. This is a personal preference, perhaps because I'm left-handed, but the other way works nearly as well for me. But for instructional purposes let's assume the rope is eye-spliced to the left D-ring of a Decker saddle as you face the horse.

To tie a basket hitch pull a generous loop of rope away from the attachment point to go around your load. Put the free end through the other D-ring from outside-in and let it drape down under the big loop you have made (step 1). Then I lift up the large loop and rest it on the top of the saddle (though you can leave it down and bring it up later around the load, rather than down). At this point, I lift the load and rest it on my stomach in the diaphragm area. (I frequently joke that a "packer's shelf," a little extra girth, is handy for this stage.)

*Mule with Decker saddle rigged for basket hitch, step 1.*

While holding the load against the side of the horse or mule, I bring the loop I've made down around the load about a third of the way down from the top (step 2), then reach under to grasp the free end of the rope. I bring it toward me and pull very hard, cinching the loop around the load (step 3).

Then I bring the free rope up from underneath the load (I try to keep it centered on the bottom) and tie it to the horizontal rope with a *slipped half hitch* (step 4). This is temporary, a good enough knot to hold the load while

*Manty basket hitch, step 2: loop around first load.*

*Manty basket hitch, step 3: rope underneath pulled hard.*

*Manty basket hitch, step 4: tied off with two doubled half hitches.*

I sling the matching load on the other side of the animal, but easily loosened should the pack have to be raised or lowered. I secure the opposite load the same way and check for balance by leading the animal around for a few steps.

If all seems good, I pull the loop on the half hitch larger and tie it into a second half hitch. There are many other fine knots that can be used, some of them more quickly released, but the doubled twin half hitches have held well for me and are relatively easy to untie.

Although it's less handy, the sawbuck can also be used with the basket hitch. With the sawbuck, use a single sling rope, not attached to the saddle, around thirty feet long. Find the approximate center and create a clove hitch (chapter 1, see page 22) by making two identical loops stacked one on the other. Place the clove hitch over the front sawbuck and pull the hitch tight. Now you have two sling ropes, one running each direction for a load on each side of the horse.

Lacking a D-ring to your right (assuming we're working on the left side of the horse), simply loop the free end of the sling rope around the right sawbuck from the outside-in. Although the sling rope will have more friction around the sawbuck than through the D-ring of the Decker, this still works relatively well. Some packers loop the vertical rope on the backside of the pack down through a cinch ring, while some allow the load to swing freely. I'm in the latter camp, having found that the "give" of the free-swinging load actually helps when the pack scrapes on a tree. The load swings to the rear but usually returns to position after a few steps.

The basket hitch can also be used on a riding saddle and works especially well on one with holes in the cantle for the purpose. The US Army McClellan saddle had these, as do an increasing number of modern backcountry saddles. My saddle, from Rick Erickson of Ennis, Montana, features these holes in the cantle. I don't feel them while riding, so they cause no discomfort, though I'm often asked about that.

As with the sawbuck, when hitching to such a riding saddle, find the center of a long rope and tie a clove hitch at that center point to the saddle horn. Then it's simply a matter of creating the large loop and threading the end of the rope back through the hole in the cantle from outside in, then proceeding to hitch the load as described. Lacking the hole in the cantle, the entire cantle can be encircled from rear, around and down.

*Riding saddle rigged for basket hitch using clove hitch on horn.*

This works, especially if the riding saddle is fairly high backed.

A riding saddle that does not have such holes in the cantle but is intended for frequent service as a packsaddle could be modified by addition of heavy D-rings located just behind and to the side of the cantle. You'd need to tell the saddle maker of the intended use so he or she would reinforce the attachment appropriately, because with a heavy load, the strain on the D-ring could be considerable.

The D-ring would have to anchor securely to the tree of the riding saddle. Then, you'd simply thread the free end of the hitch rope through the D-ring from outside in to create the hitch.

## Mantied Loads

The basket hitch works extremely well with *mantied loads*. The word "manty," adapted from the Spanish word for blanket, is a handy one, serving as both a verb and a noun. "To manty" means to tie a bundle in a particular way using a manty tarp. The word also names the bundle itself as well as the completed load.

*Author with mantied packs.*

During my lifetime in south-central Montana, I've seen the Decker/manty method of packing grow in popularity among those who frequent the backcountry. Now it's a little less common to see traditional packers with sawbucks, panniers, and diamond hitches tied neatly around tarps that cover the entire load, though many still do it that way, and the skill and knowledge of these packers is to be emulated and preserved.

Perhaps the growth in the Decker/manty method is due to its versatility. Nearly anything can be mantied, and with some loads, such as duffle bags or backpacks, you can sometimes forgo the manty tarp, simply basket hitching them directly to the Decker packsaddle. Although assembling a bunch of miscellaneous items and packing them neatly into a bundle intended to be transported on the back of a horse or mule over hill and dale may seem intimidating, mantying a load that stays together is relatively simple.

The process starts with a piece of canvas approximately seven feet by eight feet. An outfitter I know, tired of purchasing expensive canvas for his large string of mules, began using orange plastic irrigation dam material, and said it held up fairly well. Canvas, though, is traditional and nicer (perhaps especially for me, because in the course of irrigating a ranch I use all too much of the plastic). Also, natural materials always seem more appropriate and easier on a horse wherever they contact an animal's skin.

Canvas manty tarps can be hemmed or unhemmed; on some of ours we've added grommets so that they can double as easily-tied tarps for cooking shelters and such. We also use them in camp to cover our saddles, and they make good ground cloths under tents or sleeping pads.

It's good to practice mantying with something simple, such as a bale of hay. But building a load of miscellaneous items is not difficult. Place items diagonally on the tarp, laid out on the ground. Create a stack of gear approximately thirty to forty inches long, perhaps sixteen to twenty inches wide, and around a foot thick (step 1).

Manty, step 1.

Bring the bottom of the tarp up (step 2), then each side, and finally the top down, over the load (step 3). In my workshops, I've noticed many women are particularly neat at putting manties together, perhaps because they've shouldered more of the gift-wrapping duties at Christmas time.

It's easier to build a good manty if you avoid many small items, placing them instead in bags or boxes. When that's difficult, I try to place a tent pole or other rigid object on each side of the load within the manty and perhaps on top

*Manty, step 2.*

*Manty, step 3.*

as well. I've cut small saplings for the purpose in the past. When you basket hitch the load to the Decker, these will prevent your sling rope from tending to cut the manty in half by pushing down between items when the pressure of the manty ropes is applied.

It also works well to build the manty on a piece of plywood approximately eighteen inches by thirty-six inches, which tends to keep small items in place and create a neat platform for the bundle. I've also used open-top plywood boxes built for me many years ago by a friend. These are well-built of half-inch plywood and measure thirty-six inches long by sixteen inches wide and ten inches deep. The friend who built them had worked for the US Forest Service and found this size accommodated most pieces of gear they used, including folding woodstoves. Because their tops are open, the boxes aren't restricted to cargo ten inches tall, but I've found it best not to let items protrude too much above the top; slimmer manties ride better.

I've also added three hardwood legs, easily removable with bolts and wing nuts, so that one of the boxes doubles as a table in camp. For more than twenty years now, these boxes have bounced off trees and taken other sorts of abuse, and they're still serviceable.

The manty ropes are distinct from the sling ropes. Sling ropes hitch your load to the pack-saddle. These stay on the saddle. Manty ropes tie the manty into a bundle and play no part in holding the load on the packsaddle, and since their role is different, they can be lighter weight. I make manty ropes about thirty-five feet long of three-eighths-inch poly rope. Normally I build an eye splice into one end and a back splice in the other (we'll look at these in chapter 7, see page 158), but a honda knot would work as well as the eye splice.

To tie the bundle you've created, make a large lariat-like loop by threading the end of the manty rope through the eye splice or honda and encircle the bundle you've folded into the manty tarp lengthwise (step 4). The eye splice should be at the top of the manty,

*Manty, step 4.*

with the free end of the rope coming through it and down into your hands (not the reverse way). So, when you pull, you have a 2:1 leverage.

I pull the manty up toward vertical and bounce it several times to cinch it very tightly, and holding that tension I throw a loop into the free end of the rope. I invert this loop and place it over the bundle, thus creating a half hitch (step 5). I pull this tight, keeping the half hitch centered on the front of the manty (step 6).

*Manty, step 5: forming first half hitch.*

*Manty, step 6: half hitch formed on manty.*

Holding tension, I do this a couple more times, then circle the remaining free end under the manty, up its backside and around to the front to tie it off. Several knots can be used; I use two half hitches, the top one being a slip hitch, but with the end of the rope passed through the loop so that it won't inadvertently untie if it snags on something (step 7).

When basket-hitching the manty to the packsaddle, height of the packs is important.

*Manty, step 7: ready to sling.*

Assuming loads that are relatively consistent in weight (no heavy or light end), you want the manties high enough that the packsaddle, not the animal's ribs, is bearing most of the weight. Yet, too high, and the loads can become top-heavy and even flip up on the animal's rump, should he spook or jump a log. I once had that happen while packing a big gelding named Major, and it occurred in a bad place, on a ledge trail. His Decker, relieved of some of the weight on one side, then began to slip to the other.

It was a dicey few minutes, but I managed to get the load back in place and the saddle straightened on Major's back, my heels all too close to a drop-off. At the next clearing, I lowered both manties, which, with the basket hitch, is easy to do. And that's another beauty of this system. Should one manty end up, in spite of your best efforts, a bit heavier than its mate, simply sling it a little higher than the lighter pack on the other side of the horse. By doing so, given the shape of the animal's back, you shift the load inward toward his center of

*Mule with manties basket hitched.*

gravity, giving it less leverage downward, thus "lightening" the load on that side.

The packer who knows this basic system—manties, basket hitch, and (preferably) Decker packsaddle—is very well equipped, even if he or she never learns more. It's versatile, simple, and reliable. And the basket hitch can be used in other ways as well. When we're packing with panniers, either soft ones or the bear-proof, hard-sided panniers now required in so many wilderness areas, I don't stop when the panniers are hung from the packsaddle and attached by a strap underneath. I increase the security of the setup by building a tight basket hitch around the panniers as well. The hitch stabilizes the loads, prevents excessive swing, and keeps the panniers tucked up neatly. That said, it's always good to learn more, and there are occasional loads that don't lend themselves too well to a basket hitch.

## Barrel Hitch

An example would be a load that lacks a relatively square or flat bottom on which to place the base of the vertical rope holding the hitch. A hind quarter of an elk is one such load. Another relatively simple hitch, the barrel hitch, is easy to tie and handy for a load that will be held horizontally on the animal.

The barrel hitch starts with the sling rope attached the same way to the saddle; for familiarity, let's say the front Decker ring as you face the left side of the pack animal. (Again, as with the basket hitch, you can tie the barrel hitch with a sawbuck by using a long rope

*Mule with Decker saddle rigged for barrel hitch.*

tied in its center with a clove hitch to create a sling rope for each side.) Now, we'll create two loops instead of one. Keeping a loop of rope perhaps a couple of feet deep, insert the end of the sling rope back through the left D-ring from outside in, then over to the right D-ring and down. Leave another loop and bring the rope back through the right D-ring from right to left. Now you have two loose loops to go around your load.

Most packers prefer to barrel hitch with the front of the load slightly higher than the rear.

When the load's adjusted properly, the free end of the hitch rope is normally brought down to the extra cinch ring (most packsaddles have this) and tied off.

The world of horse and mule packing is not only a fascinating one, it's a liberating one. There's no need to attempt to master it all at once, because you can continue to learn more your entire life. But these relatively simple hitches and knots will get you started in the right direction. And there's nothing like clasping the lead rope of your front pack animal and heading up the trail toward campfires and yellow aspens—toward adventure. Packing your comfortable camp with you, heading into beautiful country, is one of the finest bursts of freedom the modern world allows. Once hooked, you'll be there for life.

# 5. Webbing Woes

As the years pass, changes evolve in the construction of outdoor and equine gear. A century ago rope was rope, mostly twisted and made of natural materials. But in our time, web straps, particularly those made of nylon and other synthetic materials, have become increasingly common. "Latigo" originally meant a strap made of latigo leather, but today

*A typical narrow synthetic strap.*

the strap that hooks to the cinch on your saddle (and the "billet" on the other side of the saddle) may be made of nylon rather than leather.

Narrower webbing is used on panniers, backpacks, and the straps that connect packs under the horse's belly. And, tough as these synthetics are, they occasionally fail, are unintentionally cut, and perhaps need to be joined in some way. And there's the rub.

Take two scraps of one-inch webbing and attempt to join them together with a square knot. You may succeed, but you may find that the knot slips under pull. If it doesn't slip, you'll find it difficult to untie. In any case, the flat webbing makes an ugly knot, because the material must inevitably make strange twists and turns in the course of tying. Knots imply round material—rope—and they've developed through the centuries for use on such, not on flat straps.

Enter mountaineers, who deal with webbing constantly and whose lives frequently depend on the reliability of knots. Although most of their techniques go beyond the scope of this book, one knot they frequently use can be of great help to the horseman who must join two web straps together. It's important to note, though, that climbers aren't often worried about untying the knots they create; their big concern is strength of a knot, and the rock anchors they create often are designed to stay in place.

## Water Knot

The *water knot,* also known as the *overhand bend*, can be used to join two web straps of the same width with a neat, strong attachment. Tie a loose overhand knot in the end of one of the straps (step 1). Then thread the end of the second strap into that knot by following the exact pattern of the first knot (step 2). It's easier than it sounds.

There will be some slippage while the knot is tightening (step 3), so it's important to tie the water knot with plenty of extra length in the protruding ends. These will shorten as the knot tightens.

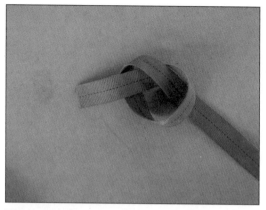

*Water knot, step 1.*

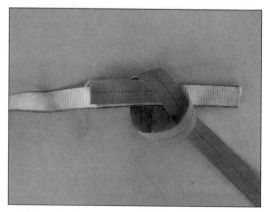

*Water knot, step 2.*

The *overhand on a bight* is another simple webbing knot, useful for attaching a web strap around a tree or other object. Again, the caveat is that it won't be easy to untie should that become necessary. To tie, just form a bight (loop) near the end of the webbing and tie an overhand knot with this loop. Wrap the resulting loop around the tree or other object, bring the end of the webbing back through it in lasso fashion, and pull it tight.

This approach can be used with rope as well, of course, but a honda knot or eye splice serves better and is easier to untie.

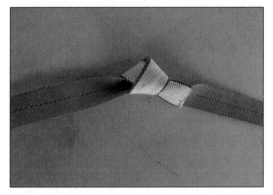

*Water knot, step 3.*

# 6. HORSE CAMP KNOTS

Ropes, knots, hitches, and splices play a big part in making a comfortable, safe camp. For me, mention of a horse camp invokes wood smoke, black coffee, horses and mules munching, aspen groves, and a bubbling creek. But, of course, there are other enjoyable types of horse camps, including more sumptuous ones set up next to living quarter horse trailers at developed campgrounds. These, too, can be satisfying, and knowledge of knots and hitches can be equally useful in these more domestic surroundings.

Most of us have a mental image of the perfect wilderness campsite: a clearing with grass for the horses, a creek for water, trees for shelter, and perhaps a beautiful view of mountains or a valley. My gelding Little Mack, now retired, has firm opinions on this. Ride him up a drainage he hasn't seen for a decade and he'll "rein himself" into the campsite he remembers. And, if you've decided not to use that location, Little Mack will take it upon himself to choose one! His judgement is quite good.

But the days when you could simply turn your animals loose in this idyllic spot are pretty much gone. Some packers still do that, usually with mules dependent on a "bell mare," a mare they've accepted as leader. Her bell tells the morning wrangler her location; he has kept a reliable saddle horse tied in camp. With this horse, he retrieves the mare, and the mules follow her to camp. But few locations are so remote that you can handle a string this way without fear it will mix with someone else's animals and perhaps disturb a neighboring camp.

This leads to the need to restrain or confine your animals in camp. Tying to trees, at least for very long, is a "no-no," and illegal in some areas. Horses and mules tend to paw when confined for long, and that cups out the area under the tree and sometimes exposes the roots. Also, some animals like to eat the bark off the tree. Such damage is unsightly and difficult or impossible to repair.

## Highlines

A highline has become the method of choice for many, and in some areas, it's almost the only alternative. One wilderness area near our ranch completely forbids grazing, which rules out even picketing and hobbling. Luckily that's not typical, and I've always questioned the wisdom of such regulations, because the result is heavier use by pack animals—pack strings must pack in their own feed, usually weed-free hay or pellets, which requires more animals and thus creates more impact.

It's rough (though not impossible) to rig a highline without trees, so we'll assume your idyllic camping spot has a couple of them, ideally twenty to fifty feet apart. My highline rope has an eye splice at one end, so I can loop it around most anything by passing the free end through the eye splice. But really you should use some sort of "tree-saver" to preserve the bark. A cinch off one of the packsaddles can work, but isn't ideal. Too often, small bits of bark work into the cinch and must be removed, and tree-sap on a cinch is less than desirable.

I know a man who makes tree savers out of rejected auto seatbelts, and commercial tree savers are also available that have a large ring on one end and a smaller one on the other. Encircle the tree, pass the small ring through the large one, and pull tight to cinch to the tree. Try to install the tree saver above a small limb or knot to lessen the chance it

*Tree-saver for highline.*

will slip down. On my highline, I insert the eye splice through the ring and the other end of the rope through the ring on the tree-saver or else tie it with a bowline. That end of the highline is the non-adjustable one.

On the other end, I pull the rope hard through the ring, and holding the slack, tie a slipped half hitch, then a doubled half hitch for security. But should I need the highline tighter than I can get it that way, I use one of the picket line loops to create extra leverage for pulling the highline really tight.

*Horse and mules on highline with metal loops.*

## Picket Line Loop

The highline needs loops to which you can tie the lead ropes of your animals. You can buy commercial metal attachments, which eliminate the need for knots, and they work well. But they aren't really necessary. Your highline rope will be lighter and easier to pack if you instead rely on a knot called the *picket line loop*. Yes, you could simply grab a loop of rope and tie an overhand knot with the

*Picket line loop, step 1.*

doubled rope and create a loop, but I wouldn't recommend it. When pressure is put on such a knot by tightening the highline and by the

*Picket line loop, step 2.*

*Picket line loop, step 3.*

activities of restless horses, you'll have a very difficult time getting the knot untied.

I do know folks who use an overhand knot as described, inserting a small stick within it. To untie they remove the stick and the knot comes loose. But the picket line loop is a better choice; it's easy to tie and usually not that difficult to untie after pressure. Turn the rope over to make a loop as shown (step 1). Then bring the right-hand portion down so it goes across in front and below the top of the loop (step 2).

Then bring the bottom of the loop up through the opening between the right-hand

*Picket line loop, step 4.*

portion of the rope and the top of the loop, pulling it tight (step 3). Start with a good-sized loop, perhaps a foot in diameter, because by the time you tighten the knot, pulling on the loop and on each side of the picket line, the loop will shrink considerably in size (step 4).

## Dutchman

To create what's called a Dutchman, a device that gives mechanical advantage for tightening the highline, tie one of these picket line loops several feet from the tree, put the end of the highline through the ring on the treesaver or cinch, then bring it back through the picket line loop. You've now created a block and tackle with a 2:1 mechanical advantage when you pull back toward the tree. Again, tie a slipped half hitch with another doubled half hitch on top of it.

Of course, there's a question of whether a highline needs to be violin-string-tight. I don't think so. It's more important that it be high enough that the horses stay under it. I space the tie loops about six feet apart, and I make sure each horse is tied short enough that it can't encircle a neighbor and twist their lead ropes together. Also, remember to tie them with some sort of swivel in the lead. Obviously, you should never tie a saddled animal to a highline. A saddle horn caught on the highline could create a major wreck.

Invariably the highline will tend to loosen during your stay, and the Dutchman system described makes it easy to tighten it

*Dutchman for tightening highline, shown here with steel picket line loop, but works as well with picket line knot.*

periodically. Animals can get testy with each other on highlines. Tying a dominant horse to one of the end loops decreases his chance to disrupt the others, and in some cases, you may have to leave an empty space between the bully and the next animal. I occasionally hobble a horse on the highline to discourage excessive pawing and the damage to the ground it causes.

Even if the horses don't paw excessively, during an extended camp stay the ground under a highline is likely to become trampled and disturbed. Building the highline on high, rocky ground can lessen the impact, but if possible, move the highline periodically. When you break camp, scatter manure and use your camp shovel to level the disturbed ground, repairing any damage as best you can.

Where grazing is allowed, hobbling and picketing become practical methods of horse restraint. Training for both hobbling and picketing by the front foot were discussed in chapter 2 (see page 39). Normally you'll use a hobble half for picketing to a front foot (on a horse so trained). Do not picket with a rope to the halter. It's dangerous, should the horse spook or fall. There's also a chance the horse can catch a hind foot in its halter while reaching up to scratch, and that can be disastrous.

Even while the animal is picketed by a front foot or hobbled, the halter should be removed and kept in camp so your horse won't catch a hind foot in that fashion. There's another benefit too. When a horse isn't tied, he's free to try all sorts of tricks to rub his halter off. If he loses it in tall grass, you're short a halter.

## Tying a Rope Halter

But if you lose a halter, all is not lost, even if you've forgotten to include an extra in your packed gear (always a good idea). You can make a lariat loop-type halter with a piece of rope. Tie a honda knot in one end and create a loop that goes over the horse's head and rests on his poll, behind his ears. Then insert a half hitch around his nose, as shown on the next page. This halter works well for leading

*Rope halter, bowline around neck with full twist around nose.*

an animal, but is dangerous for tying because it will tighten around the poll should the horse pull back. In effect, this type of halter creates something similar to a "war bridle," a high-leverage halter that should be used only for careful training, not for tying.

For a rope halter safer to use for tying, I'd tie a loop around the top of the animal's neck with a bowline, then make a loop around its nose by twisting the rope twice. Pulling back will result in some tightening above the nose, but there's less chance of strangling the animal or hurting the sensitive nerves in the poll area.

## Hobbles

As with halters, hobbles can be improvised if lost. Of the separate types, those made with rings that attach in a figure eight pattern are too easily lost unless they're attached with most slack taken out. And, in tall grass or snow, they're difficult to find. When I use this type, I plant the horse's front feet closely together, not only to prevent loss of the hobbles but to limit the horse's movement.

The material of which these hobbles are made is also important. Nylon hobbles are light, impervious to moisture, and inexpensive, but I avoid using them on animals that are likely to resist and be overactive in hobbles. Leather is kinder to the skin.

Don't count on the limitation to movement hobbles are supposed to impose. A few horses I've owned never really figure out how fast they can move in hobbles, but the majority soon discover they can hop, then actually gallop with their front feet hobbled. Indeed, I once had a young walking horse that actually jumped fences while hobbled. In order to utilize grass around the homestead, I'd hobbled him here and there and kept spotting him on the wrong side of the fence. Finally, I caught him in the act. He'd approach the fence, square up with it, rear back, and jump! Had he been a mule I'd have been less surprised.

Partner, my senior gelding, runs like the wind while hobbled, and I fear for his safety on rough ground. I've seen him tear along on a rocky side hill in order to find the next spot of green grass. The solution for him has been three-legged hobbles.

On one of my earlier pack trips I took two young sons twelve miles up a familiar drainage and camped in what westerners call a "park," a big, beautiful clearing high in the timber. This clearing was a favorite with horse people, because to reach it you crossed a narrow bridge over a river that would be nearly impassable without it. Since horses normally didn't attempt to cross the treacherous river

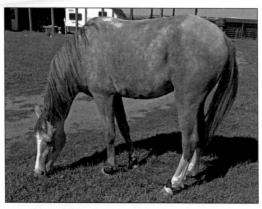

*Three-legged hobbles.*

willingly, all one had to do to hold horses in camp was place a pole across the bridge entrance, and a pole was always left there handy for that purpose.

The boys and I rode over the bridge, then up the path a couple hundred yards to the clearing. We made camp, ate Polish sausages, and watched a young cow moose graze in the south end of the big clearing, only occasionally raising her head to check us out. Young and foolish as a packer, I had hobbled all of our horses.

After supper, I told the boys we should go down to the river and brush our teeth, and, while we were there, place the pole across the bridge. We skipped down and did so, then hiked back up to camp and built a fire. That action, putting the pole across the bridge, probably saved us a twelve mile walk back to the trailhead.

Just before dark, Mona, our senior Tennessee Walking Horse mare, who knew this drainage well from years of service with a wilderness outfitter, suddenly threw her head into the air, snorted, and decided it was time to go home. She took off in a fast hop down the trail, and the others, seeing "Mama" move, followed suit. We dropped what we were doing and sprinted after them, quickly learning that even a hobbled horse could outrun any of us.

We caught up with them at the bridge. Mona, still leading, her front feet on the first of the bridge planks, her chest against the pole, was stopped dead, a disappointed look on her face. I snapped on a lead rope, removed her hobbles, and led her back to camp, her young charges following. There, I tied her securely to a dead but solid tree.

Since this incident, I have never hobbled all my horses. Keep one reliable horse tied fast. Otherwise, a long walk might be in the offing. And it reinforced for me the meaning of an old mountain man's saying: "Better to count ribs than tracks." In other words, better to let your tied horse be deprived of feed during the night than to see only his tracks the next morning. And on this memorable pack trip with my sons, "ribs" weren't of concern: the horses were fat from a spring on green grass.

But in spite of their limitations, hobbles are an essential part of the backcountry horseman's inventory of gear. In addition to providing some restraint for horses, you can use them to minimize the turf-damaging pawing of a horse anywhere you happen to tie him. And should you lose a pair, you can improvise with any piece of rope, particularly a soft one (like cotton) of fairly large diameter.

As always when hobbling, work to the side of the horse, never in front. Reach your rope

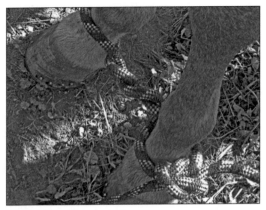

*Rope hobbles with square knot.*

around the opposite pastern, bring both sides of the rope back, and twist three or four times. Then move the horse's near foreleg close to the other, bring your rope around, and tie a square knot around its pastern.

(Always hobble on the pasterns, never the cannon bones, where fragile tendons can be damaged. Some tack catalogs show otherwise, but they're wrong, just the same.) As long as you've provided enough twists to take up the space between the horse's legs, these hobbles are fairly secure.

*Attach to the pastern, not the cannon bones, when hobbling or picketing.*

## Pickets

For holding horses in the backcountry while still allowing them to graze, the next step up in security is picketing by one front foot, only done with horses well trained to yield each foot when restrained (as discussed in chapter 2, see page 39). My picket ropes have an eye splice in one end and a back splice with crown knot in the other (which we'll practice in the next chapter). The eye splice can be used either to permanently enclose a swivel snap, or you can just slip the loop through the ring on the snap, then the snap through the loop and pull tight. That way the snap can be easily removed. On the end attached to the picket stake, I usually tie a bowline.

I've used two types of commercial picket stakes. One, of aluminum, came with a bull-snap with swivel attached, but the snaps were of low quality and broke readily. My current ones are much heavier, but are longer, are made of sturdy steel, and have a swivel on top to which to tie.

But a picket rope can be attached to a big rock or downed log, too, and the eye splice is then handy to use as a lasso around the object—just put the end of the rope through the splice and pull to take out the slack. Then attach your hobble half to one front foot. Always lead the horse out to the end of the picket rope so that he knows he's restrained. You don't want him to take off quickly and hit the end of it hard. Shown his limitations, he'll settle down to graze.

To be light on the land, move picket stakes frequently. Otherwise, the horse will graze an unsightly circle.

## Transom Knot

In some areas it's permissible to cut poles for camp, but where that's not possible, you are usually allowed to construct temporary camp conveniences with downed timber. Nails and wire are frowned upon, but it's possible to build a hitching rail using rope lashings alone.

*Transom knot, step 1.*

These don't do permanent damage, and you can disassemble and scatter your materials at the end of the stay.

The *transom knot* is a simple one for holding a horizontal pole against a tree or another vertical pole. Loop the rope around the vertical pole up above the horizontal one (step 1), then down and under itself (step 2).

Then bring the other end around the vertical pole below the horizontal one, over the first rope, and under the two loops you've

*Transom knot, step 2.*

*Transom knot, step 3.*

made (step 3). Then pull both ends to tighten the knot. Two poles tied horizontally at the same height between two trees with transom knots, overlaid with a piece of plywood (should you have used one as a backing for a manty) make a nice table. All can be disassembled afterwards, "leaving no trace."

## Sheepshank Knot

Particularly when setting up tents, perhaps using an extra guyline for further strength, you may find the rope you have on hand is excessively long. We use manty ropes for this purpose, and we certainly don't want to cut them. A knot called the *sheepshank* is a way to shorten a rope without damaging it.

Make a fold in the rope which shortens it to the length you want. In doing so you've created two bights, one on the left and one on the right (step 1).

On your left in the standing part of the rope, twist to make a half hitch, and slip it over the end of the bight (loop) on the left (step 2). Now do the same on the right, slipping the second half hitch over the bight on that side (step 3). Now slowly tighten the rope.

Do be aware that this knot will only hold as long as pressure is applied. If the rope goes completely slack, the sheepshank can come untied. Thus, the sheepshank is not an appropriate method for shortening a picket rope or highline, a rope that's likely to be jerked around by horses and allowed to go slack, and then be tightened again. But it's very handy for a static, temporary use.

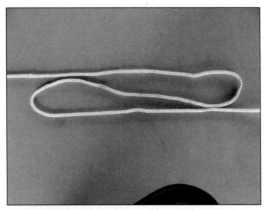

*Sheepshank knot, step 1.*

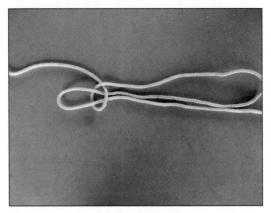

*Sheepshank knot, step 2: half hitch around bight.*

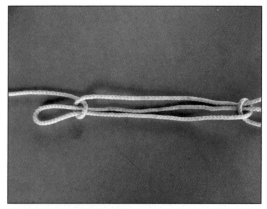

Sheepshank knot, step 3: half hitch around the other bight and pull tight.

More and more of our wilderness areas require storage of food either in bear-proof containers or hung overhead a given distance from tree trunks. Often this requires both an overhead line between two trees, then another to hang the food container (perhaps a light cooler) over the horizontal line. We usually use manty ropes, and the *sheepshank* is a handy knot for shortening them to the needed length, avoiding extra line lying round ready to trip you in the dark.

## Taut-Line Hitch

Equally handy around camp, especially for setting up tents, is the *taut-line hitch*. It's especially useful for guy ropes on a tent, because it can be slipped to adjust length, then, when under load, holds fast. Tying the taut-line hitch is easy. Just bring the rope around the object (step 1), such as a tent stake, and make two wraps around the standing part *within* the loop you've created (step 2).

Then make a third outside the loop. Pull the knot together, and you'll find that under weight of a heavy load it doesn't slip. Release the pull, however, and you can adjust the line.

On a recent backcountry trip, I ran a long guyline from the peak of my tent to a large stump, knowing the prevailing winds from that direction might be severe that evening. I used a taut-line hitch with some trepidation, knowing the winds would be fickle, blowing the tent back and then releasing it in many sequences. But the hitch held fine. (Certain other things about the tent setup did not, but that's another story.)

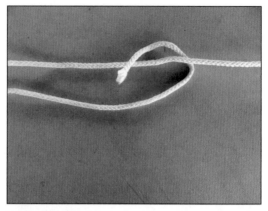

*Taut-line hitch, step 1.*

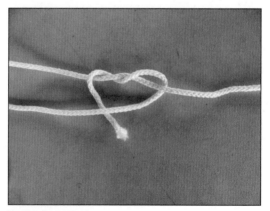

*Taut-line hitch, step 2.*

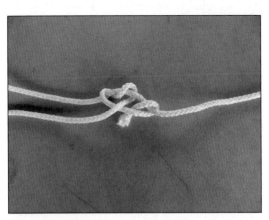

*Taut-line hitch, step 3.*

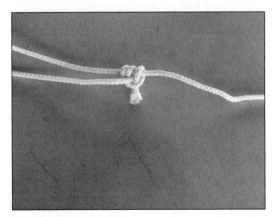

*Finished taut-line hitch.*

# 7. SIMPLE KNOTS AND SPLICES

## Eye Splice

The *eye splice* is the first one I'd recommend learning, because it's handy in so many ways. You can use it to make a lead rope, to make a loop at the end of a picket rope that's easily attached to a rock or tree—just pull the end of the rope through the loop around the object—and you can improvise a lasso with it should one be needed.

It's easy to make an eye splice with three-strand rope. Just unravel six inches or so and loop the intact portion of the rope around into the size eye splice you want (step 1).

It can be helpful to put a wrap of electrical tape around the standing portion of the rope as a divider between it and the unraveled portion. The tape prevents additional unraveling while you're working. And, if you're using a natural fiber rope, you might want to put a

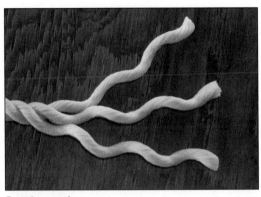

*Eye splice, step 1.*

wrap of tape around the end of each unraveled strand to make them easier to insert under strands of the standing portion. With synthetic rope you may wish to burn each end, but with care—melted synthetic strands can be dangerously hot until they cool.

First insert the middle strand of those you've unraveled under one strand of the standing portion (step 2). This first tuck determines the size of the "eye." Then rotate the rope to one side and insert the second strand over the same strand but under the next (step 3).

*Eye splice, step 2.*

*Eye splice, step 3.*

Then rotate back to the third strand, which goes under and over the strand previous to (toward the standing part) the one under which you tucked the first strand. After that it's a matter of weaving the ends alternately over and under strands as you work your way up the rope (step 4).

If you mess up, it will be evident; the splice will lose its nice, round look. Just pull out a few strands, backing up, and start again. It's easier than it sounds.

*Eye splice, step 4.*

When you're all done, rolling the splice on a hard floor under your shoe gives it a finished touch. The splice is amazingly strong after the unraveled strands have been tucked four or five times. With natural fiber rope, four tucks of each strand are probably plenty. Synthetic rope is more slippery, however, so five or six tucks are a good idea

The very same procedure can be used for splicing two three-strand ropes together, creating a much nicer connection than merely tying them. Splices were always preferred on sailing ships because a neat splice can run through a pulley block. The procedure is the same as we used for the eye splice, but now we unravel the ends of each rope for six or eight inches. Again, tape or burn the ends of each strand (depending on the type of rope) to hold them together and make threading them through the standing portions of the rope easier, and put a wrap of tape around each rope to prevent further unraveling.

Now place the two ropes together end to end, mating their unraveled strands, placing them so that the intact portions are touching. Tape the two together at this point. Now proceed to splice one of the ropes to the other by the very same method you used for the eye splice, alternating tucks over and under into the solid portion of the adjoining rope. When you've completed going in one direction, go in the other. Finally, roll the splice under your boot and trim off any strands that protrude. For synthetic ropes, half a dozen tucks in each direction will do the trick.

Such a splice is amazingly strong. As kids, we used to buy what were called Chinese handcuffs or finger traps. Younger kids were encouraged to insert their fingers in each end of these woven tubes. Upon pulling, the tubes tightened and held their fingers fast. The strength of a spliced rope is similar. Pressure tightens all the woven strands upon each other. The strength is nearly that of an undamaged rope, and the splice is much neater than any knot that could similarly join the two ropes. It's comforting to know that if a mishap requires you to cut a sling rope on your packsaddle (because a horse or mule is down, perhaps, with the sling knot underneath it) you could repair the rope with a splice in very short order.

## Lead Ropes

To add to the techniques learned so far, we can make lead ropes out of any three-strand rope, making them as long as we wish, with or without adding a snap. I like to make them at least ten feet long, so starting with a piece of rope eleven to twelve feet long is about right. For a permanent snap, we simply insert the end of the rope through the ring on the snap, then weave an eye splice containing it in the loop. Do make sure you purchase bull snaps or sliding snaps that have swivels built in. I recently pulled a bull snap off my shop wall, still in its packaging, and found it had no swivel. For a lead rope such a snap is useless.

But sometimes it's preferable to simply tie in an eye splice without a snap. Now, as mentioned earlier, you have an option.

When you wish to use a snap, merely poke the end of the eye splice through the ring on the snap (step 1), and then insert the snap back through the loop of the eye splice (step 2).

The connection is secure (step 3), and the snap can be easily removed.

If you prefer to ride with the lead rope attached to a halter under your bridle, leave the snap off. Insert the eye splice through the ring on the halter and bring the other end of the lead rope through the eye splice, pulling

*Attaching bull snap to eye splice, step 1.*

*Attaching bull snap to eye splice, step 2.*

*Attaching bull snap to eye splice, step 3.*

the whole rope through. Such a connection is quiet, free of the metal-on-metal sound of a snap, and also light and less likely to interfere with your horse's neck rein. If you intend to tie the horse to a highline you'll need a swivel, so throw a snap with swivel into your saddle bags for attachment as described above, later in camp.

But how about the other end of the lead rope? We can leave it plain, perhaps burning the end (if it's synthetic) to prevent unraveling, or if it's natural fiber rope, learning one of the methods of whipping. An expedient is simply a wrap of tape around the end of the rope.

But I like to finish my lead ropes with something more attractive and useful on the end. Occasionally a horse pulls a rope through your grip when you're not ready for it, and I find a back splice on the end helps one grip at the last moment, preventing loss of the rope. Yes, you could tie a stopper knot at this point, but that might interfere with inserting the rope through a loop such as that on a highline. The back splice is constructed with the same technique we use for the eye splice and short splice, but in order to start it correctly we need to tie a crown knot in the end of the rope.

## Crown Knot

To tie a crown knot, which will lead into a back splice, unravel six inches or so of rope (step 1). Pick the center strand (strand 1) and fold it down into a loop (step 2).

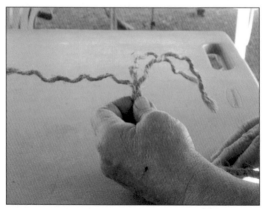

*Crown knot, step 1.*

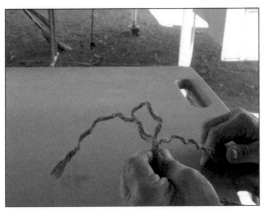

*Crown knot, step 2.*

Pick the strand to its right (strand 2) and wrap it around the loop you've made (step 3), making sure it stays on top of the one remaining unraveled strand (strand 3).

Then insert that last strand through the loop you first made, above strand 2. To complete the knot, gently pull on each strand in turn, gradually tightening it (step 5).

The crown knot inverts the unraveled strands, facing them down toward the intact portion of the rope. Now it's a matter of

*Crown knot, step 3.*

*Crown knot, step 4.*

starting the back splice by choosing any strand and tucking it over and under, as with the eye splice. The pattern is the same, and when completed you have a nice "handle" at the end of the rope, preventing it from unraveling but also giving you something to grip should the rope pull through your hand. It looks good, too, and is compact enough to slip through halter or highline rings if needed.

This sort of lead rope is so easy to make that the backcountry horseman should consider building a spare to hang in the horse

*Turning a crown knot into a back splice.*

trailer and to take on a pack trip. They're also easy to join together should a longer rope be needed; just insert the back spliced end through the eye splice of the other rope, then through its own eye splice and pull the rope through. Now you have an extra twenty-foot rope.

Similarly, short lengths of spare rope, three or four feet long, with an eye splice in one end, will prove handy for a host of duties around the horse trailer and tack shed. Making some up is a great rainy day project. You'll find a host of uses for them around your camp and on your horse, whether for quickly securing an object to a tree or pole, tying a jacket on your saddle using a D-ring, or a quickie, short lead rope for moving your horse from high-line to hobbles.

# CONCLUSION: LIFELINES

I write this shortly after returning from a pack trip into the wilderness north of Yellowstone National Park. After twenty years of applying, I drew a mountain goat tag. Perhaps it came too late in life—I'm certainly not of an age or physical condition to tackle nearly vertical slopes looking for creatures that laugh at lung-aching altitude or scramble up sheer cliffs needing only suggestions of ledges to bound their way to the top.

No matter. When an opportunity comes, you take it and be thankful for it. And, after guiding a friend to a goat years earlier, I knew that the animals sometimes frequented the bottoms of those cliffs, not always the top. And more important, a wilderness quest is a "hunt" enough in itself. So, the tag was an excuse to go, but to go with a goal in mind— to look hard for mountain goat, but enjoy the challenge and not be disappointed if I came home without one.

And it went just that way. My friend Billy and I saw mountain sheep, but no goats.

*Author in the wilderness.*

The surroundings were spectacular: a rugged ridge that formed the border of Yellowstone to our south, a panoramic wall of rock with timber patches below, green yet, but with white patches of early fleeting snow. The horses and the mules behaved, and for the most part our packing skills proved themselves. Each day we rode taking just one lightly packed animal with us to relieve the burden of excessive gear strapped to our saddle horses.

There were thrills each day, the primary ones supplied by a ghost grizzly that we never saw but whose tracks and scat appeared fresh in new places every morning, often overlaying our own tracks from the previous day. The presence of an animal whose strength dwarfs one's own is to us more reward than threat, but it's a reminder that in wilderness you aren't necessarily at the top of the food chain. There's a tingle on the back of your neck at the first sight of fresh grizzly tracks, and we hoped to see him, but at a safe distance. At one point the horses continually eyeballed a patch of timber to our right. They didn't snort or spook, but they matched our attitude of watchfulness. We proceeded carefully, but the grizzly remained concealed.

In camp, there was good food, too much of it, and the companionship always furnished by a good buddy and our equine friends, the horses and mules that munched the pellets we gave them and enjoyed their turns grazing on the picket ropes. And there was time to reflect on this book and the importance of its contents, because everywhere I looked there was a rope of some sort, fulfilling a certain purpose, used with one of the appropriate knots or splices.

Billy had furnished his highline, complete with commercial tree-savers. Because the highline featured manufactured (and very handy) picket line loops made of steel, no such loops needed to be tied into the highline itself, but I was able to use one of the metal rings to construct a Dutchman to tighten the line. The horses and mules were tied to the highline with lead ropes whose snaps were attached within eye splices, their ends featuring a crown knot and back splice.

Our picket ropes were made with a heavy snap within an eye splice on one end, and a large eye splice on the other that allowed encircling a prominent rock, lasso fashion. Our tent was tightened with the usual guylines, and the slip-line hitch worked well, allowing simple adjustment without untying.

On the trail, we packed three animals, each with separate techniques. Beauty, the big mule, carried the commercial certified bearproof food panniers, stout plastic boxes of a model that had withstood testing by a hungry bear. We could have simply hooked the boxes to the Decker saddle, then tied the belly strap under Beauty's stomach, but we supplemented that packing job with a tight basket hitch.

Two heavy manties containing pack boxes went on a mare named Tess. These, too, were held in place by basket hitches. Zorro, our smaller mule, got the easiest load, two cloth panniers filled with the items we'd first need in camp or on the trail.

In many respects, when it comes to handling equines, ropes and knots are lifelines, connection between the animals, the object, and our own hands. Learning knots that are outside our comfort zone is a pleasure, and it can expand throughout our lives. Yes, the average horseman can probably get along simply knowing the square knot, half hitch, and bowline. (The first I'd add to that collection would be the sheet bend.) But there are many more knots and hitches to be learned, ones that are tailor-made for particular purposes, and it's worth going after them.

In this book, I've made no attempt to teach as many knots as possible. Why? Quite frankly, because most readers will quickly forget knots to which they are exposed simply by reading a description, viewing a diagram, or by watching an online animation. These things do not make one proficient at tying knots or at choosing the right knot for a particular job.

Nowhere more than in tying knots is the expression "use it or lose it" more appropriate.

We remember the knots we use. Pushing the envelope involves practicing them and judiciously adding others as time goes on.

Once I asked a mushroom expert to tell me the best approach to gathering mushrooms without poisoning oneself. A professor at my graduate school had recently died, poisoned by a mushroom he mistook for another. The expert answered that it was simply a matter of learning one at a time and really learning it. Don't worry about the others, he told me. Become proficient at identifying one safe species, and then consider adding another.

If this book has only accomplished teaching you to tie a square knot, making you aware that you've been tying a granny knot instead, that's good progress. But the next time you're tempted to tie two lines together with a square knot, tie a sheet bend instead. It's a better knot for that purpose, and the more you tie it, the more natural it will seem. Or, for fun, join the two lines together with two bowlines, loop to loop, even though that kind of strength isn't necessary for your purpose.

Practice tying the knots you find most useful behind your back or in the dark. Keep a couple strands of colored rope next to your computer, and when you find yourself a little bored, pick them up and challenge yourself to tie one or more of the knots in this book. Eventually you'll acquire a fluid, unthinking motion that results in the knot you wish to tie.

A marine biologist who was an accomplished sailor once came to the ranch for my "Beyond the Round Pen" clinic. This man knew more knots than I'll ever be able to tie, and he could tie a bowline blindfolded, in the dark, and underwater. When I split up the class and asked him to teach the bowline to his section he tried for a time, and then, exasperated, said, "I can tie it, I just can't teach anyone else to do it!"

That's not an uncommon development with knots, a momentary setback when you find you can't tie a knot that was completely natural to you. But it's not a bad one. The biologist had simply reached a proficiency level in tying the bowline that had long left behind the actual steps involved. He was "overthinking" the situation when asked to teach.

But that sort of proficiency is what you're after. When you find you've tied a bowline without thinking of its steps, you've reached something akin to proficiency in a foreign language, when you no longer must translate a sentence, but just say it naturally.

Develop the knots you need, add a few as you learn them (like the mushrooms), and really learn them. You and your horses will be happier and safer.

Happy Trails!

# GLOSSARY

**Artificial or manmade rope:** Synthetic fiber rope such as nylon, Dacron, polyester, or polypropylene.

***Ashley Book of Knots:*** The accepted "Bible" of knots, containing nearly four thousand of them.

**Bear-proof panniers:** Hard-sided panniers usually made of plastic or metal that have been certified by the US Forest Service to protect food from animals, primarily bears. Required now on many public lands.

**Bend:** A category of knots, such as the sheet bend, for joining two lines together.

**Bight:** A loop in a rope or line.

**Billet:** Strap on off side (right) of a western saddle that attaches to the cinch.

**Bone:** Size of bone structure in comparison to weight; at least seven-inch circumference of front cannon bone is desirable for one thousand pounds of weight.

**Breakaway system:** Halters and lead ropes intended to release the horse should he pull back; a wrong-headed development that can train a horse to strain against the lead rope.

**Breeching:** More commonly pronounced "britching" or "britchin'," the arrangement of straps that go over the rump of the pack animal to hold the load back on downhill grades.

**Bull snap:** A rugged metal snap with a tongue that swivels outward rather than slides.

**Cantle:** The rear portion of the saddle rising behind the rider's seat.

**Cinch:** Also cincha and girth; a wide strap of web or neoprene that goes tightly under the horse's rib cage to secure a saddle.

**Crossbuck:** Packsaddle also known as sawbuck.

**Crupper:** Sometimes pronounced "crouper," a strap that encircles the base of a horse's or mule's tail to help prevent slippage of the saddle and load forward.

**Dally:** One or more wraps around the saddle horn used when ponying another horse or dragging something from the horn.

**Decker packsaddle:** A packsaddle originally designed to carry ore and mining equipment; consists of two wood bars joined by iron D-rings covered with a "half-breed" pad filled with horsehair or foam.

**Diamond hitch:** A type of packing hitch used to secure a top pack on a pack animal, so named because in most of its configurations the hitch rope forms one or more diamond-shaped patterns.

**Dutchman:** A system for tightening a line by running it through a loop and back, creating 2:1 leverage.

**Eye splice:** A splice which creates a loop at the end of a line.

**Grass rope:** Common western term for a rope of natural fibers.

**Half-breed pad:** A padded covering on a Decker packsaddle containing two horizontal boards to help distribute the weight of the pack and protect the animal from odd-shaped objects.

**Highline:** A tight line strung overhead with loops to which attach the lead ropes of restrained horses or mules.

**Hitch:** In the packing world, a system of ropes and knots designed to hold cargo on a pack animal.

**Hobble half:** A strap with buckle and ring to attach to just one pastern for picketing or other purposes.

**Hobbles:** A strap or rope normally between the front pasterns of a horse or mule to prevent excessive movement; three-legged hobbles have an additional strap that extends from a ring between the animal's front feet back to a hobble half on one hind pastern.

**Honda:** The eye of a lariat through which the loop runs.

**Latigo:** Both a type of leather and the strap on the left side of a western saddle, used to secure the cinch.

**Lay of a rope:** Refers to the direction of twist in a rope. Most are of right-handed (clockwise) lay.

**Manty:** The Spanish term for blanket, refers to a tarp in which a load can be assembled for a pack horse, and also refers to the completed pack. As a verb, to manty means to build such a load.

**Manty rope:** A light rope, normally three-eighths inch, used to secure a manty (bundle) within its tarp.

**McClellan saddle:** The standard saddle of the US Army from the Civil War through World War II; the seat is relatively deep, the pommel lacks a saddle horn, and the cantle has holes through which sling ropes can be threaded. Replica McClellan saddles are still popular, and they double well as packsaddles.

**Natural fiber rope:** Rope made of cotton, hemp, manila, flax, or other naturally grown organic fibers.

**Neck rein:** Technique of riding in horses properly trained for the trail that allows riding with just one hand, the reins gently moved in the direction the rider wishes the horse to turn, the horse responding by turning correctly, cued only by the feel of the reins against his neck.

**Packer's scale:** Usually a spring-type scale with a top handle and hook below, set up to stick at the maximum point of stress so the packer can weigh a manty or pannier, then read the weight before releasing the indicator.

**Panniers:** An old French word (Shakespeare used it) for bags or boxes secured on each side of a packsaddle to carry cargo. Sometimes corrupted to "panyards."

**Pastern:** The portion of a horse's foot just above the hoof but below the first joint (fetlock).

**Picketing:** Restraining a horse with a long line, often tied to a stake and secured to a horse's front pastern.

**Poly rope:** Slang for a rope made either of polyethylene or polypropylene.

**Pommel:** The front portion of a saddle; in western saddles, the portion holding the saddle horn.

**Reef knot:** Another name for square knot.

**Remuda:** A group of horses tradition-ally assembled in a corral before work. Cowboys then roped their mount to be used that day.

**Running knots:** Knots designed to allow movement of one of their components, such as a slip knot or honda knot.

**Saddle panniers:** Cloth bags with appropriate slits to fit over a riding saddle when it must double as a packsaddle.

**Saddle strings:** Usually leather thongs attached to the saddle, made for tying objects onto the saddle.

**Sawbuck packsaddle:** A wooden packsaddle consisting of two wood bars joined by wooden cross members in an X pattern.

**Sheets:** The lines (ropes) on a sailboat that adjust the sails.

**Sling ropes:** Ropes on packsaddles for attaching cargo.

**Snubbing post:** Traditionally, a solid post in the middle of a corral to which to tie or wrap a lariat rope when an animal had been roped.

**Splice:** An attachment of two ropes together or another to itself, as with eye splice.

**Standing portion:** The part of the rope that leads into the knot.

**Stopper knots:** Knots such as the overhand knot intended to be tied in the end of a rope for grip or to prevent unraveling.

**Tackaberry:** A hook with buckle that attaches to the ring of a cinch, making it faster to saddle and unsaddle, since none of the latigo leather needs to be threaded or unthreaded through the ring.

**Tapaderos:** Sometimes abbreviated to "taps," stirrup covers that if well designed would prevent a foot from sliding all the way through a stirrup and possibly hanging up.

**Tree-saver:** A strap to encircle a tree and prevent damage to the bark when attaching a highline.

**War bridle:** A type of rope halter made to tighten on the horse's poll (area just behind the ears on the top of the neck).

**Whipping:** A system of wrapping string or thread around the end of a rope to keep it from unraveling.

**Withers:** Conformational feature of horses, refers to point at base of neck; the tallest point on a horse when its head is down to eat grass. Helpful in holding a saddle.

# INDEX

Page numbers for main entries and instructions are in boldface.

_____

_____

_____

_____

_____

_____

_____

_____

_____

_____

_____

_____

_____

_____

# NOTES